British Aircraft Manufacturers since 1908

Half-title:
Designed and built in six months, the Avro York military
transport used Lancaster wings, engines and tail unit with the
addition of a central fin. Production amounted to 350, and a
number went to BOAC and smaller airlines.

British Aircraft
Manufacturers since 1908

Günter Endres

IAN ALLAN
Publishing

Contents

First published 1995

ISBN 0 7110 2409 X

Published by Ian Allan Publishing

an imprint of Ian Allan Ltd, Terminal House, Station Approach, Shepperton, Surrey TW17 8AS.
Printed by Ian Allan Printing Ltd, Coombelands House, Coombelands Lane, Addlestone, Weybridge, Surrey KT15 1HY.

Front cover:
G-ACSS, the third DH88 Comet to be built, won the speed section of the 1934 England to Australia air race. It is preserved at the Shuttleworth Trust. *BAe*

Back cover:
Jaguar strike aircraft. *BAe*

Title page:
Although it was the RAF's first four-engine bomber, the Shorts Stirling did not enjoy the popularity of the Halifax and Lancaster. Its low service ceiling and inability to carry the larger bombs, because of the bomb bay configuration, were against it, but the 2,209 delivered to the RAF performed a useful service, later versions excelling in glider towing. A further 160 were built as long-range transports. *M. J. Hooks Collection*

Bibliography

C. F. Andrews and E. B. Morgan, Supermarine Aircraft since 1914. Putnam
C. H. Barnes, Handley Page Aircraft since 1907. Putnam
Charles Gardner, British Aircraft Corporation.
Bill Gunston, World Encyclopaedia of Aircraft Manufacturers. Patrick Stephens
E. A. Harlin and G. A. Jenks, Avro: an Aircraft Album. Ian Allan
A. J. Jackson, Avro Aircraft since 1908. Putnam
A. J. Jackson, Blackburn Aircraft since 1909. Putnam
A. J. Jackson, British Civil Aircraft since 1919, Vols 1, 2 and 3. Putnam
A. J. Jackson, De Havilland Aircraft since 1915. Putnam
Derek N. James, Hawker: an Aircraft Album. Ian Allan
Jane's All the World's Aircraft. Jane's Information Group
Jane's Encyclopaedia of Aviation. Jane's Information Group
Jane's Fighting Aircraft of World War II. Jane's Information Group
Francis K. Mason, Hawker Aircraft since 1920. Putnam
James D. Oughton, Bristol: an Aircraft Album. Ian Allan

Foreword

British aircraft manufacture is approaching its 90th anniversary. It was in the summer of 1907 that Alliot Verdon Roe began constructing his Roe I biplane, achieving several hops before making the first recognised flight by an Englishman in an aircraft of his own design at Brooklands on 8 June 1908. Soon after the first company set up specifically to build aeroplanes, was registered. World War 1 provided an upsurge in the demand for military flying machines, and unforgotten men like Geoffrey de Havilland, Thomas Sopwith and others came up with the aircraft that could engage in aerial combat with an enemy the country was to face again 25 years later. After the first battle was won, great airliners and sporting aircraft largely supplanted military biplanes and monoplanes until the mid-1930s when renewed threats again filled factories with thousands of war machines. Among them were such types as the Supermarine Spitfire, Hawker Hurricane and Avro Lancaster, which will forever retain a special place in the hearts and history of the British people.

Although many companies struggled and some succumbed to economic pressures between the wars and after 1945, peacetime could never extinguish the entrepreneurial spirit that has distinguished the aircraft manufacturing industry in Britain. Unfortunately, bungling governments often could and did, and today, Shorts and British Aerospace are all that is left of a once proud and prolific tradition. Shorts, while now flourishing under foreign ownership, no longer builds complete airframes, and British Aerospace's future is closely bound up in collaborative ventures with European partners. It has no new indigenous aircraft projects on the drawing board, and the continual changes in strategy and lack of clear direction, do not bode well for the future. In today's economic climate, it is unlikely that from the fast diminishing band of small enterprises, aircraft will emerge once again, that are a true reflection of British expertise and design genius. It is, therefore, from the past that we need to find that spark of enthusiasm and remind ourselves of the men and machines that gave Britain a place in the skies among the best.

Günter Endres
Sussex
February 1995

Introduction

The British aircraft manufacturers described in this book reflect a broad history of nearly nine decades of prodigious output, shaped strongly by two world wars. It is not intended to be a definitive and all-embracing review — with many great designers and manufacturers deserving several volumes of their own — but rather to provide a quick reference guide to place on the bookshelf alongside other historic tomes. Space limitations prohibit the mention of every prototype and production aircraft of each manufacturer, so the author has, therefore, chosen to restrict coverage generally to the most important or interesting subjects. For the same reasons, manufacturers of airships, gliders, microlights and gyrocopters have had to be omitted, as are those companies that produced only foreign aircraft under licence rather than indigenous designs. Aircraft built at the bottom of the garden by individuals, rather than companies, also had to be left out. A few aircraft whose design or production was taken over by a succession of different companies are listed under the original manufacturer, although details of their subsequent vicissitudes are provided within the same entry.

The author would like to acknowledge with gratitude the valuable assistance of Mike Hooks, who provided almost all of the expert captions to a great selection of 250 photographs, which amply illustrate the sheer breadth, ingenuity and success of British aircraft design since the very beginnings of heavier-than-air flight. He also read the text, ensuring that there were no serious errors and omissions. Photographs have been provided from the archives of Ian Allan, Mike Hooks, Philip Jarrett and the author. As few of the manufacturers reviewed in this book are still in existence, liberal reference has had to be made to many other excellent publications, without which it would have been near impossible to complete British Aircraft Manufacturers Since 1908 to the high standard expected from the reader.

ABC

Producers of piston engines, ABC Motors Ltd of Walton-on-Thames, Surrey, built one single-seat cabin monoplane, designed by A. A. Fletcher and known as the ABC Robin. It first flew in June 1929 at Brooklands, powered by ABC's 40hp Scorpion engine, but was scrapped in 1932.

AIRCO

The Aircraft Manufacturing Co Ltd was established at The Hyde, Hendon, by George Holt Thomas in 1912, but did not start aircraft production until midway through 1914 when Geoffrey de Havilland joined as chief designer. De Havilland's first design for Airco was the DH1, a two-seat reconnaissance biplane powered by a single 70hp Renault inline engine. This was soon replaced by the 120hp Beardmore, which resulted in the DH1A. An urgent requirement for a high-performance single-seat fighter led to the DH2, again a pusher, but fitted with a Gnome Monosoupape engine and first flown in July 1915. Some 400 were built and were followed by the DH3/3A bomber, de Havilland's first twin-engined design, and the very fast and successful two-seat DH4/4A day bomber (1,449 built), first flown in August 1916. Civil DH4s

were used on cross-Channel services in 1919. The single-seat DH5 was designed in 1916 as a replacement for the DH2 and featured a backward stagger of the upper wing to provide the pilot with improved forward vision of the pusher-engined aircraft.

De Havilland's later fame for designing superb training aircraft began with the two-seat DH6, of which more than 2,280 were built. The DH9 of 1917 was a replacement for the DH4 and was further developed into the DH9A, which became one of the outstanding strategic bombers of World War 1. In the immediate postwar years, it was used extensively on pioneering air services. The only other types to be built by Airco were the DH10 Amiens, a three-seat heavy bomber, powered by a pair of Rolls-Royce Eagle or American Liberty engines, and the four-seat DH16 and eight-seat DH18 airliners, operated by Holt

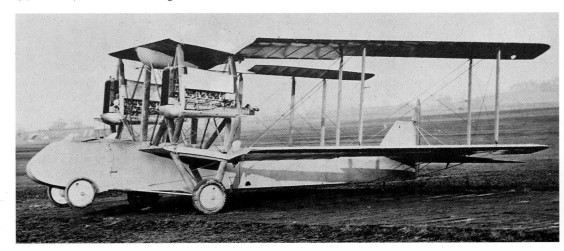

Left:
Almost 6,300 de Havilland DH4s were built in over 60 variants with 22 different engines; of these, more than 4,800 were manufactured by five US companies. O-BARI was a cabin conversion, one of four operated by the Belgian airline SNETA on cross-channel routes.

Below:
Designed to replace the DH4, the de Havilland DH9 was developed into the DH9A (illustrated) with various engines in the 375-465hp range including the Rolls-Royce Eagle and American Liberty.

Left:
Aircraft Transport & Travel operated the prototype de Havilland DH18 from April to August 1920 when it was wrecked in a forced landing. The other five built were used by Instone Air Line.
Samson Clark

7

Thomas' own and Britain's first airline, Aircraft Transport and Travel Ltd. But with military orders cut drastically and the British Government's short-sighted decision not to support the fledgling civil aviation industry, Holt Thomas' companies were forced into liquidation in 1920. Their assets were bought by the Birmingham Small Arms Co (BSA), which had no intention of taking over the aviation activities.

Airspeed

The first aircraft to be produced by Airspeed Ltd, established by A. H. Tiltman and N. S. Norway in York, was the AS4 Ferry, designed in 1932 for pleasure flying to Sir Alan Cobham's specification. It was an exceptionally large three-engined wooden biplane with Gipsy engines and could carry 10 passengers.

Tiltman then incorporated modern design concepts in the six-seat AS5 Courier cabin monoplane, the first British type with flaps and a retractable undercarriage, using a hand pump mechanism. The Courier made its first flight on 11 April 1933 at Portsmouth, where Airspeed had moved into larger premises and was then reformed as Airspeed (1934) Ltd when it became associated with the famous Tyneside shipbuilding firm of Swan, Hunter & Wigham Richardson Ltd. This was quickly followed with a stretched twin-engined development, designated the AS6 Envoy, which saw service with a number of airlines and air forces after 1934.

The AS10 Oxford was designed to an Air Ministry specification and flew for the first time on 19 June 1937. The Oxford became the RAF's first twin-engined cantilever monoplane trainer when it entered

Above:
The Airspeed Courier, of which 16 were built, was normally powered by an Armstrong Siddeley Lynx or Cheetah engine (240-277hp) but this example was used to test the 325hp Napier Rapier IV engine.
M. J. Hooks Collection

Left:
The prewar Czechoslovak Airlines (CSA) employed four Airspeed AS6E Envoy IIIs, mainly on the Prague–Moscow service, inaugurated on 2 September 1936.

service with the Central Flying School in November that same year. More than 8,500 were eventually produced in five main versions for military use, and Airspeed converted some 160 surplus airframes into a commercial six-seat light transport, redesignated as the AS65 Consul, between 1946 and 1948. During the war, Airspeed also built nearly 3,800 AS51 Horsa I and AS58 Horsa II military gliders, whose most famous hour came during the D-Day landings. The AS39 Fleet Shadower, designed for shadowing enemy naval vessels during hours of darkness, and the AS45

Top:
The attractive AS57 Ambassador had a short life, entering service only a year before the turboprop Vickers Viscount. After being retired from British European Airways in 1958, many found their way to charter companies, where they were used as passenger and cargo transports.

Above:
The Airspeed Consul was a postwar conversion of surplus Oxford airframes and could carry six passengers. It filled a useful gap until more modern equipment became available. *M. J. Hooks Collection*

Cambridge advanced two-seat trainer, remained in prototype form only. The AS57 Ambassador, first flown on 10 July 1947, was an attractive 47-seat high-wing monoplane with distinctive triple fins, retractable nosewheel undercarriage and two 2,700hp Bristol Centaurus engines. Twenty operated with British European Airways as the 'Elizabethan' class between March 1952 and July 1958. Airspeed, which had been acquired by de Havilland in 1940, became the Airspeed Division in 1951.

Below:
The two-seater P2 Seabird biplane was designed in 1919 by J. A. Peters for the Atlantic competition, but failed to make an impact. Only two were built, distinguished by rear undercarriage radius rods on one, and front radius rods on the other. *Philip Jarrett Collection*

Alliance

The Alliance Aeroplane Co Ltd of Acton, West London, built two aircraft types immediately after World War 1. The first, designated P1, was a redesign by J. A. Peters, of the Ruffy-Baumann RAB15, following the take-over of the Ruffy, Arnell and Baumann Aviation Co, based at Hendon. This two-seat trainer bi-plane, powered by one 80hp Renault engine, was given a horn-balanced rudder and improved undercarriage in 1919, but was scrapped in November 1920. The more powerful P2 Seabird, another two-seater but with a 450hp Napier Lion engine, was built to its own design in 1919 for competition flying with an intended endurance of 21hr. Only two were completed and one crashed on 13 November that year, killing both pilots.

ANEC

In the years after World War 1, W. S. Shackleton designed a small number of wooden ultralight monoplanes, all built at Addlestone, Surrey, by the Air Navigation & Engineering Co Ltd, which had succeeded the wartime Bleriot & Spad Manufacturing Co in 1919. The first aircraft was the high-wing ANEC I, fitted with the 696cc Blackburne Tomtit modified motorcycle engine, the first inverted engine to fly in the UK, which made its maiden flight at Brooklands on 21 August 1923. Two further examples were built with a 1,100hp Anzani engine, which also powered the first ANEC II, a scaled-up two-seater and Shackleton's last design for ANEC before joining William Beardmore Ltd. J. Bewsher then designed the ANEC III, a large transport for use in Australia, and the two-seater ANEC IV Missel Thrush biplane, designed for the 1926 Daily Mail competition and the last aircraft to be built.

Armstrong Whitworth

Sir W. G. Armstrong Whitworth & Co Ltd was founded in 1897 from the merger of two rival engineering and shipbuilding firms and moved into aircraft production with the approach of World War 1. During these early years, the company built BE2a/b and BE2c fighters at Elswick Works, Gosforth, Newcastle-upon-Tyne, followed by a number of its own types originated by its chief designer, Frederick Koolhoven. Among these were the FK3 two-seat reconnaissance and training biplane in 1915, the larger FK8 in 1916, and the FK10 two-seat fighter/bomber a year later. Armstrong Whitworth also built 250 Bristol Fighters and several airships, the latter at Barlow, Selby. The purchase of the Siddeley Deasey Car Co Ltd in February 1919 resulted in a move to Coventry and the reorganisation into Armstrong Siddeley Motors Ltd, and Sir W. G. Armstrong Whitworth Aircraft Ltd, which established a factory at Whitley Airfield and later at Baginton, both in the Coventry area.

Under new chief designer John Lloyd, two military types of note were produced in the immediate postwar years, including the diminutive Armstrong Siddeley Jaguar-powered Siskin fighter biplane, which entered RAF service in 1924 taking over from the Sopwith Snipe, and the larger Atlas, first flown on 10 May 1925, specifically designed for the army co-operation role. The 1923-vintage 25-seat Awana troop transport and two-seat Wolf reconnaissance biplane were unsuccessful. Armstrong Whitworth then built three airliner types for Imperial Airways which, although produced in small numbers only, made a significant impact on the airline's Empire routes. The first to fly, on 16 March 1926, was the Argosy, a 20-passenger biplane fitted initially with three 385hp Jaguar air-cooled radial engines. It entered service on 16 July 1926 and was followed into service on 26 September 1932 by the AW15 Atalanta, a high-wing cantilever monoplane with four 340hp Armstrong Siddeley Serval III engines and accommodation for 17 passengers. The company's third airliner type was the AW27 Ensign, like the Atalanta a high-wing four-engined aircraft, but of all-metal stressed-skin construction and seating for up to 40 passengers. It first flew on 24 January 1938 and a total of 14 were built at Air Service Training Hamble, another

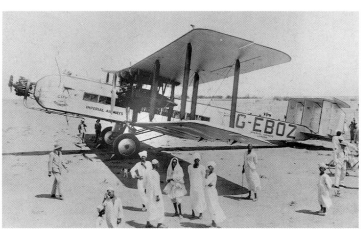

Above:
Around 480 Armstrong Whitworth Siskins were built and served with 11 RAF fighter squadrons between 1924 and 1932. A dual-control trainer version was used at Flying Training Schools.
M. J. Hooks Collection

Left:
Initially used by Imperial Airways on European routes, some Armstrong Whitworth Argosies were later transferred to Cairo where they operated to Khartoum with an overnight stop at Aswan.
British Airways

member of the Hawker Siddeley Aircraft Co Ltd, of which Armstrong Whitworth Aircraft had become a founder member in 1935.

The factory at Whitley was working flat out producing the AW38 Whitley heavy bomber, which had first flown on 17 March 1936 and entered RAF service in March 1937. The twin-engined AW41 Albemarle was initially designed as a reconnaissance bomber, but was later produced as a glider tug and troop carrier. Wartime production also included large quantities of Lancasters, Lincolns, Stirlings and Barracudas, and postwar, the company took over development and manufacture of the Hawker Sea Hawk, Gloster Meteor night fighter, and built 133

Gloster Javelins. Own postwar designs included the unsuccessful AW55 Apollo, a 30-passenger transport aircraft powered by four Armstrong Siddeley Mamba turboprops, and the AW650 Argosy civil and military twin-boom passenger and freight transport, which entered production as the Hawker Siddeley HS650 Argosy. The AW52 was an interesting tail-less research aircraft, which first flew on 13 November 1947. The major reorganisation of the Hawker Siddeley Group into Hawker Siddeley Aviation and Hawker Siddeley Dynamics on 1 July 1963 resulted in the Avro Whitworth, later Whitworth Gloster Division, with the original names finally disappearing on 1 April 1965.

Right:
Armstrong Whitworth's Atalanta was designed for African routes, but its first services were to Brussels and Cologne in September 1932. The attractive lines were in strong contrast to the Argosy, but the streamlined spats were later discarded.
M. J. Hooks Collection

Below:
Britain's largest prewar airliner was the Armstrong Whitworth Ensign, of which 14 were built. Although it gave useful service, the type was expensive to operate and keep serviceable. The example shown is in wartime camouflage with red, white and blue stripes underlining the registration. *British Airways*

Arpin

In 1937, M. B. Arpin & Co designed and built a two-seat, twin-boom, cabin monoplane at West Drayton, Middlesex, designated the Arpin A-1. Only one aircraft was built and was first flown at Hanworth by G. Wynne Eaton on 7 May 1938. This rather odd-looking aircraft was fitted with a pusher engine and had a McLaren crosswind tricycle undercarriage. It was scrapped in 1946.

Above:
The best known Armstrong Whitworth product was the Whitley heavy bomber. Early versions had the company's Tiger radial engines, but the majority of the 1,814 built were, as in the illustration, Rolls-Royce Merlin-powered. *M. J. Hooks Collection*

Below:
Only one Arpin A-1 was built. The rather odd-looking aircraft was fitted with a pusher engine and had a McLaren crosswind tricycle undercarriage. It was scrapped in 1946. *Philip Jarrett Collection*

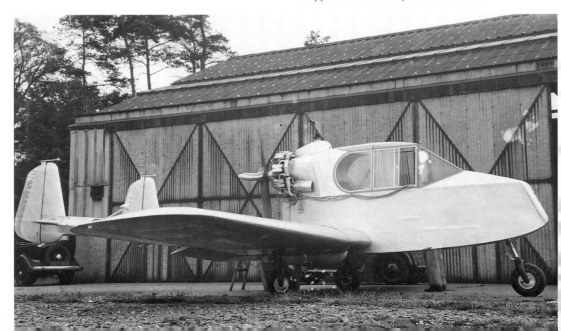

Arrow

Two single-seat, high-performance, all-metal aerobatic trainers were manufactured at Yeadon, Leeds, by Arrow Aircraft Ltd. The first was the Active 1 of 1931, powered by a 115hp Cirrus Hermes IIB, followed a year later by the improved Active 2, which differed mainly in having an additional strutted upper-wing centre section and a 120hp Gipsy III inverted air-cooled engine. Both aircraft flew in the King's Cup races in 1932/33 and reached speeds of up to 137mph. The Active 2 is still airworthy.

ASL

The Aeronautical Syndicate Ltd, founded in June 1909 at Larkhill on Salisbury Plain by Horatio Barber, was one of the world's first aircraft manufacturing companies. After an unsuccessful attempt with a tractor design, where two propellers were driven by chains from a fuselage-mounted engine, Barber designed and built some 30 Valkyrie tail-first canard monoplanes including the single-seat Valkyrie A, the lighter Valkyrie B for two passengers, powered by a 50hp Gnome engine, and the three-seat Valkyrie C.

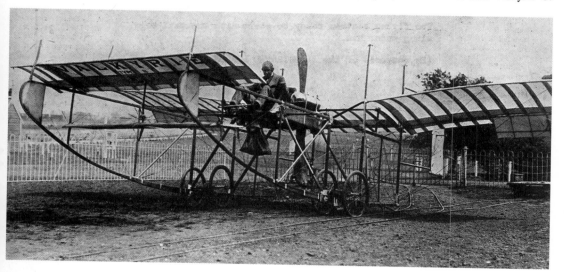

Top:
There were only two Active Arrows built. One, as illustrated here at the 1933 King's Cup race, was fitted with a 155hp Cirrus Hermes engine; the second received a Gypsy III engine. *M. J. Hooks Collection*

Above:
The ASL Valkyrie had the distinction of flying the first United Kingdom Aerial Post on 9 September 1911, for the General Post Office. The postman is seen here ready to start with the mail slung under him.

The last two were constructed at Hendon where ASL had moved to in September 1910. The Viking 1 reverted to the tractor design, but was not completed. Throughout, Barber had to fight against official antipathy towards the Valkyrie and after his retirement in April 1912, the company ceased operations.

Auster

Auster Aircraft Ltd was the successor to Taylorcraft Aeroplanes (England) Ltd, formed in 1939 to manufacture designs under licence from the Taylorcraft Aircraft Corporation of America. During the war, the company built 1,604 Auster 1, 2, 3, 4 and 5s for the RAF and Army Air Corps at its Britannia Works, Thurmaston, Leicester, for use as two/three-seat artillery spotters or Air Observation Posts (AOPs). Taylorcraft assumed the name of Auster Aircraft Ltd on 7 March 1946 and transferred its base to nearby Rearsby Aerodrome. The Auster 5 formed the basis of the civil J-1 Autocrat, J-1N Alpha and J-1U Workmaster models, which were produced in large numbers immediately after the war and had upholstered accommodation and other refinements. The two-seat J-2 Arrow followed the Autocrat into production, and a number of variants of the basic two- and three-seat airframes added to the company's portfolio. Among these were the J-1B Aiglet; the J-4, an Arrow with a 90hp Blackburn Cirrus Minor 1, replacing the American Continental engine; and the J-5F Aiglet Trainer. Auster's first production four-seater was the J-5B Autocar, built in several versions with different powerplants and used in a variety of roles, including ambulance duties and crop-spraying. A specific type for the latter application was the B8 Agricola, first flown on 8 December, 1955. An interesting earlier, albeit unsuccessful project, was realised with the B4 rear-loading ambulance freighter of 1951. Development of the new D series was continued by Beagle Aircraft Ltd after it acquired Auster in June 1961.

Left:
The AOP.9 was the final production version of Auster's series of air observation post aircraft and served with the RAF and Army Air Corps from 1955 until replaced by helicopters in the mid-1960s. Total production reached 145 and several are now operated on the civil register. *M. F. Sketchley*

Below left:
Some 100 four-seater Auster Autocars were built, powered by a 130hp DH Gipsy Moth I engine. Illustrated is an example which served with the Royal Australian Navy. *M. J. Hooks Collection*

Above:
The Auster Aiglet Trainer was the company's first fully aerobatic aircraft, and of the 70 built most were exported — a German example is shown. In a non-aerobatic role it could carry four people. *M. J. Hooks Collection*

Below:
Auster's attempt at a specialised crop-spraying aircraft was the Agricola, which could carry ¾ ton of superphosphate. Powered by a 240hp Continental 0-470 engine, it did not sell and only two were built. *M. J. Hooks Collection*

Austin

The Austin Motor Co Ltd was established by Herbert Austin in Birmingham in 1905 and went on to become one of Britain's largest car manufacturers. When the commercial chassis market slumped during World War 1, Austin tried his hand at aircraft manufacture and in 1916 built a prototype of the Austin-Ball AFB1 single-seat fighter to a specification suggested by Albert Ball, one of Britain's World War 1 fighter aces. This came to nothing and Austin followed up with the equally unsuccessful AFT3 Osprey triplane and Greyhound biplane fighters. In 1919, the company built the Whippet, a small single-seat biplane designed by John W. Kenworthy. Powered by a 45hp Anzani air-cooled radial engine, the Whippet was intended for the private flyer, but fell victim to the postwar recession. Only five were built at Austin's Northfield Works. Even less success was achieved with the Kestrel, a side-by-side two-seater biplane with a 160hp Beardmore engine, built in response to the 1920 Air Ministry Competition. Only one example was completed. After this less than encouraging venture into diversification, the Austin Motor Co returned to concentrate on its core business.

Aviation Traders

The Southend-based Aviation Traders (Engineering) Ltd, founded in 1949, embarked on an ambitious aircraft programme in the mid-1950s, focusing on the development of a 28-seat medium-range airliner with two 1,740hp Rolls-Royce Dart 512 turboprops. Known as the ATL90 Accountant I, the one and only example made its maiden flight on 9 July 1957, but further work was abandoned six months later for lack of interest. Concurrently, the company began work on civil conversions of the Percival P40 Prentice trainer, including a single seven-seat example. ATL then turned its attention to converting Douglas DC-4s into car ferries, by adding a new bulbous nose section and a hydraulically-operated, sideways-opening nose door to facilitate loading. This conversion was given the designation ATL98 Carvair, the first of which flew on 21 June 1961. A total of 21 aircraft were converted over the next seven years.

Below:
The diminutive Whippet had a fabric-covered fuselage and folding wooden wings with N-type interplane struts and steel lift struts. Shown is the second aircraft at Gosport on King's Cup day, 24 August 1924.
Philip Jarrett Collection

Right:
Freddie Laker's Aviation Traders company made a brave attempt to attract small airlines to turboprop power with the Rolls-Royce Dart-engined 28-seat Accountant, flown in 1957, but lack of interest killed the programme. *M. J. Hooks Collection*

Below right:
Conceived as a Bristol Freighter replacement by Aviation Traders in conjunction with British United Airways, the Carvair was a modified DC-4 with a hinged nose and raised flight deck, providing accommodation for six cars and up to 22 passengers.

Avro

After a short-lived partnership with J. A. Prestwich — builder of the JAP engine — Alliot Verdon Roe joined with his brother H. V. on 1 January 1910 at Brownsfield Mills in Manchester to establish A. V. Roe & Co, which was to develop into a prolific organisation. A. V. had made a few hops at Brooklands in his Roe I Biplane in 1907 before achieving the first recognised flight on 8 June 1908; flown his famous Triplane I in July 1909 and in 1912 designed the world's first totally-enclosed monoplane, but it was the 504 series of biplanes which enhanced the legend during World War 1. The 504 became the standard trainer of the Royal Air Force and, in a production spanning nearly 20 years, a total of 8,340 were built. New factories were built at Miles Platting, Failsworth, Hamble and Newton Heath, but when peace came, Avro was forced to supplement aircraft production with the manufacture of toys and sports goods. Nevertheless, the company built 35 different aircraft types between the wars, ranging from the 534 Baby and Avian light aircraft popular with flying clubs, to the Tutor which replaced the 504 as the RAF trainer and the elegant twin-engined Anson monoplane, of which more than 11,000 were produced for a variety of roles.

When, in November 1924, the Air Ministry's lease ran out at Alexandra Park Airfield in Manchester, where the company had conducted its test flying, A. V. Roe purchased land at New Hall farm at Woodford in the Cheshire countryside, starting aircraft manufacture at Woodford which continues to this day. In 1928, A. V. Roe sold his interest to J. D. Siddeley of Sir W. G. Armstrong Whitworth Aircraft, and formed Saunders-Roe Ltd. In 1935, Avro became a founder member of the Hawker Siddeley Aircraft Group and in 1938 all operations were moved to Woodford and a large new factory at Chadderton, north of Manchester. A new 'shadow' factory was also established at Yeadon. World War 2 gave birth to the Lancaster heavy bomber whose contribution to the war effort can be gauged by the fact that it was responsible for two-thirds of the bomb load dropped by the RAF after it went into service in 1942. A total of 7,366 Lancasters were built. A scaled-up version, the Lincoln, first took to the air on 9 June 1945.

Anticipating the need for commercial transport aircraft once peace returned, Avro developed the York, Tudor and Lancastrian, all based on the Lancaster. Next came the Shackleton, a maritime reconnaissance aircraft using Tudor and Lincoln components, and the awesome four-engined Vulcan, the first jet bomber to employ a delta-wing configuration. Powered by four 20,000lb st Olympus turbojets, the Vulcan made its first flight on 30 August 1952 and became the backbone of Strike Command. Five Avro 707 research aircraft were built to test the behaviour of delta wings, especially at low speeds. The medium-range 748, which became one of the best-selling British airliners, was the last to bear the famous Avro name. The company lost its identity in July 1963 when all constituents were merged into a new company, Hawker Siddeley Aviation. In 1993 the Avro name was revived by a new division of British Aerospace at Woodford.

Left:
A. V. Roe taking off in his first Roe I triplane, in which he achieved the first flight over British soil in an all-British design with a British engine, a 9hp JAP. *Avro*

Top:
Britain's first post-World War 1 practical light aircraft was the Avro Baby of 1919, which was fitted with a 35hp Green engine. Eight were built and enjoyed considerable success; one was still flying in Australia in 1936, where a replica (shown) was built recently. *R. H. Hitchins*

Above:
The Avro 504 was indisputably the most famous wooden trainer ever built and after the end of World War 1 a large number were civilianised and used for joy-riding, banner towing and charter work. There are several airworthy survivors.

Left:
Developed as a passenger aircraft for Imperial Airways, the Avro Anson served the military in many roles, from trainer and transport to bomber and reconnaissance. Shown is the last Anson built, a T.21, flying over its Woodford birthplace in May 1952. *Avro*

Below left:
Most famous bomber of World War 2 was the Avro Lancaster, with over 7,000 built. Several survive in museums and there are currently two airworthy examples — one in Canada and the other, PA474 shown here, with the Battle of Britain Memorial Flight.

Above:
The Avro Lancastrian was adapted from the Lancaster with pointed nose and tail cones and with military equipment removed. In all, 82 were built, of which 67 were British registered. Several RAF aircraft were later used as flying testbeds for jet engines, which were mounted in place of the outer Rolls-Royce Merlins.

Below:
The handsome Avro Tudor flew in June 1945 but demanding BOAC modifications eventually led to the airline cancelling its order. Later versions included the MK 4 shown in BSAA colours, but following two unexplained disappearances the type was withdrawn. Aviation Traders enjoyed some success with a number converted to freighters.
British Airways/Author's Collection

Above:
The sound of an Avro Shackleton's four Rolls-Royce Griffon engines driving contraprops is never to be forgotten. Production reached 181, and Shackletons served the RAF for 41 years before the last was retired in 1992. Sixteen were built for the South African Air Force, and one is being restored to flying condition after a first restoration was lost in 1994.

Below:
Probably the best known of the RAF's postwar bombers was the Avro Vulcan. Two prototypes were followed by 134 production aircraft and the type served the RAF from 1956 to 1993 when the last airworthy example was finally grounded.

Above:
The glider origins of the Kronfeld (originally BAC) Drone are evident in the picture. A single-seat prototype, the Planette, had a 600cc Douglas motorcycle engine, but the 58 production Drones had either a 23hp Douglas Sprite (Super Drone) or 30hp Carden Ford (Drone de Luxe). *M. J. Hooks Collection*

Below:
The British Aircraft Manufacturing Co at Hanworth built two six-seat Double Eagle aircraft, the first (illustrated) with two 130hp DH Gipsy Major engines and the second with 200hp DH Gipsy VIs. Both flew in the 1936 King's Cup race, being placed third and fifth. *M. J. Hooks Collection*

BAC

The British Aircraft Co was founded in 1928 to build a series of gliders, but in 1932 its designer and managing director, C. H. Lowe Wylde, fitted a 600cc Douglas motorcycle engine to the BAC VII tandem two-seater to produce the Planette. Two more were built, but during demonstration flights on 13 May 1933, Lowe Wylde was killed. After BAC was acquired by Austrian sailplane pilot Robert Kronfeld, he renamed it Kronfeld Ltd in 1936. Moving into larger premises at Hanworth, Kronfeld then produced 33 modified Planette aircraft with a 23hp Douglas Sprite engine, known as the Drone, before closing down in 1937.

BAMC

After Maj E. F. Stephen secured the selling rights to the popular German Klemm L25 wooden two-seater in 1933, he set up his own manufacturing plant at Hanworth, Middlesex, and began operations as the British Klemm Aeroplane Co Ltd. The first Hanworth-built version, known as the BK Swallow 1, was offered with the 75hp Salmson AD9 radial, or the 85hp Pobjoy Cataract II, and was succeeded by the Swallow 2 with still greater power. When the company name was changed to the British Aircraft Manufacturing Co Ltd (BAMC) in 1935, that aircraft became known as the BA Swallow 2. The 1934 BK1 Eagle, a side-by-side cabin monoplane with a

Left:
The FK23 Bantam single-seat biplane fighter never saw wartime service. Only nine were built and civilianised for use in racing. Designer Frederick Koolhoven took one fitted with an Armstrong Siddeley Lynx radial engine to Holland, where it is believed to have exceeded 154mph.
Philip Jarrett Collection

manually-operated outward retracting undercarriage, designed by its chief designer G. H. Handasyde, was later developed into a de luxe version under the designation BA Eagle 2. Subsequent products included the similar BA3 Cupid, and the BAIV Double Eagle, a six-seat mid-wing aircraft, powered by two 130hp de Havilland Gipsy Majors.

BAT

The Willesden, London-based British Aerial Transport Co Ltd, was a short-lived enterprise founded in 1917 by Samuel (later Lord) Waring. It built a number of designs of Dutchman Frederick Koolhoven, who had been taken on as chief designer, starting in 1918 with the FK23 Bantam, a single-seat biplane fighter powered by one 170hp ABC Wasp I radial engine. The FK27 was a more powerful two-seat aerobatic and racing variant. Neither the Bantam nor the two-seat FK24 Baboon trainer entered squadron service. After Armistice Day, BAT constructed the first civil aircraft, the FK26, which was a conventional fabric-covered biplane powered by a 350hp Rolls-Royce Eagle VIII water-cooled engine and seated four passengers in a glazed cabin. The pilot had to make do with an open cockpit in the rear fuselage. An interesting project was the FK28 Crow, an ultralight model where the pilot sat in the open under the wing. When the company closed down in 1920, Koolhoven returned to the Netherlands.

Beagle

When Auster Aircraft Ltd was acquired by British Executive & General Aircraft Ltd (Beagle), the name Beagle-Auster Aircraft Ltd was adopted for a short while from June 1961, before another retitling to Beagle Aircraft Ltd in 1962. The first aircraft to carry the Beagle name were the D5/180 Husky and the A61 Terrier. The latter was a rework of the ex-Army Auster 6B into a three-seat touring and training aircraft. A heavier, four-seat derivative had the

designation A109 Airedale, which made its first flight from the company's base at Rearsby Aerodrome, Leicestershire, on 16 April 1961. Two interesting developments came to nothing. One was the experimental four-seat composite B218X, initially known as the Beagle-Miles M218, the other the B242X, a scaled-down four-seat model of the B206, which had made its aerial début on 12 August 1962. The twin-engined B206 eight-seat light transport, was produced in Series 1, 2, 3 and 206R Basset CC1 versions, but still greater success was achieved with the B121 Pup, an all-metal aerobatic machine, which reached a production rate of one aircraft a day. Three versions were produced at Rearsby and at Shoreham Aerodrome, Sussex: the Series 1 (Pup 100) with two seats and a 100hp Rolls-Royce Continental engine, the Series 2 (Pup 150) with an optional third seat and 150hp Lycoming, and the three-seat Series 3 (Pup 160) with a 160hp Lycoming. The installation of a 200hp Lycoming engine produced the B125 Bulldog 100 trainer in 1969, but production of this model was taken over by Scottish Aviation at Prestwick, after Beagle Aircraft surprisingly closed down in 1970.

Beardmore

Dalmuir, Dunbartonshire, was the home of William Beardmore & Co Ltd, a shipbuilding and engineering concern, which moved into aviation in 1913 by building engines and aircraft under licence, including the BE2c. G. Tilghman Richards then designed a series of two-seaters, including the WBI bomber, WBII fighter with a 160hp Beardmore engine to replace the BE2c, and the 185hp WBX, all flown in 1920. The WBIII was a development of the Sopwith Pup for use on board ship, distinguished by its folding wings and landing gear. Fifty-five served with the Royal Navy. This led to the WBIV and WBV naval fighters and in 1925, W. S. Shackleton designed the WB26 tandem two-seat fighter for Latvia. An Air Ministry contract followed for two Inverness flying

Top:
The Beagle Basset was the RAF version of the B206 light executive twin with 310hp Rolls-Royce Continental G10-470 engines. Twenty were built, some replacing Ansons from mid-1965.

Above:
Beagle's most successful product was the all-metal Pup, produced with Rolls-Royce Continental or Lycoming engines. Designations 100, 150 and 160 indicated the engine horsepower; this is a Pup 150. When Beagle went into voluntary liquidation in 1970, 128 Pups had been built and there were 267 outstanding orders. *Beagle/M. J. Hooks Collection*

boats and one giant landplane bomber, the Inflexible, both types all-metal aircraft using the Rohrbach stressed-skin construction. The Inflexible, powered by three 650hp Rolls-Royce Condor IIs, first flew on 5 March 1928. With a wingspan of 48m, it was the largest British landplane prior to World War 2. Beardmore also built seven other civil prototypes, successfully participating in the 1924 Lympne Light Aeroplane Trials with its WBXXIV Wee Bee 1, a two-seater with a single 32hp Bristol Cherub engine.

Blackburn

Civil engineer Robert Blackburn started designing monoplanes as early as 1909, including the single-seat monoplane No 1 and two-seat Mercury, and set up his own company, Blackburn Aircraft Ltd, in June 1914, winning subcontract work to build the BE2c and Sopwith Baby fighters and Sopwith Cuckoo torpedo-bomber at Olympia, Leeds, and nearby Sherburn-in-Elmet. Like Richard Fairey, Blackburn concentrated mainly on naval types from then on,

Above:
The Mercury was the third aircraft built by Robert Blackburn. Powered by a 50hp Isaacson radial engine, it was a two-seater and flew early in 1911. The picture shows it at Filey, with Blackburn's hangar on the right and the slipway down to the beach.
Hawker Siddeley Aviation Ltd/M. J. Hooks Collection

Below:
Blackburn's Kangaroo long-range bomber was used for World War 1 anti-submarine patrols from North Yorkshire. Around 20 were built with Rolls-Royce Falcon engines, and 11 of these were subsequently converted for civil use in freighting and pleasure flying.
Flight/M. J. Hooks Collection

Above:
The Blackburn Bluebird was the first British side-by-side two-seater to enter production and 79 were built in various marks with engines ranging from 80 to 100hp. G-EBSW was a Bluebird II which made Round Britain and German flights in 1928, attending the Berlin Air Show.
Hawker Siddeley Aviation Ltd/M. J. Hooks Collection

building a succession of carrier-based torpedo-bombers and civil and military flying boats. Starting with the RT1 Kangaroo in 1918, the T1 Swift, T2 Dart, T3 Velos, T5 Ripon and its successor the B5 Baffin, and the B6 Shark followed in the next 15 years. All were single- or twin-seat biplanes, powered mostly by Napier Lion water-cooled engines. The most prominent flying boats of the interwar years were the elegant five-seater RB1 Iris with 675hp Rolls-Royce Condor IIIA engines and RB3A Perth coastal patrol boat with 825hp Rolls-Royce Buzzard IIMS engines, while the two-seater Bluebird series, beginning with the L1 Bluebird I of 1924 and ending with the L1C Bluebird IV in 1929, were landplanes. Other landplanes included the F2 Lincock single-seat biplane of 1928, the B1 Segrave four-seat cabin

Top:
Replacing the Ripon's water-cooled engine with a radial led to the Blackburn Baffin of which B5 was the second prototype with a 545hp Bristol Pegasus. This engine was selected for production aircraft and 15 were built with a further 62 Ripons converted to Baffins. *Doughtys Ltd/M. J. Hooks Collection*

Above:
The Blackburn Skua was the Fleet Air Arm's first operational monoplane and the first purpose-designed British dive-bomber. It entered service with No 800 Sqn on HMS *Ark Royal* in November 1938. Two prototypes and 190 production aircraft were built. *Aeroplane*

monoplane and the B2 side-by-side all-metal biplane trainer. All were built at Leeds and a new factory at Brough, to the west of Hull.

Wartime production comprised large numbers of Fairey Swordfish and Barracuda torpedo-bombers, and Short Sunderland flying boats at Dumbarton on the Clyde. Its own prominent designs were the B-24 Skua dive-bomber, first flown on 9 February 1937 and 190 delivered by March 1940, and the B-26 Botha, which, although a failure as a torpedo-bomber, served successfully as a multi-role trainer. The B-37 Firebrand torpedo-bomber only entered limited service after the war. In January 1949, Blackburn Aircraft acquired General Aircraft and developed the four-engined GAL60 Universal freighter into the B101 Beverley, which served with RAF Transport Command until 1967. Other activities included licence-production of the Prentice and Balliol trainers, and concluded with the design of the NA39 Buccaneer low-level strike/attack aircraft which first flew on 30 April 1958. Unfortunately, Blackburn Aircraft was not to reap the benefits of what proved to be an outstanding aircraft, being taken over by Hawker Siddeley Aviation in 1960 and operating briefly as the Hawker Blackburn Division before losing its identity completely on 1 April 1965.

Boulton Paul

Norwich-based engineering firm, Boulton & Paul Ltd, set up an aircraft department in 1915 when it obtained a contract for the construction of the FE2b fighter aircraft, followed by other subcontract work. Its own first design, created by chief designer J. D. North, was the P3 Hawk, later renamed the Bobolink, which lost out to the Sopwith Snipe as a Camel replacement. Immediately after the war followed the P6 two-seat wooden biplane and the slightly larger P9, and the P7 Bourges twin-engined two-seat day bomber. After J. D. North had switched from wooden to all-metal designs with the follow-on Bolton, Bugle and Bodmin, he created a series of high-performance

Above:
Blackburn's largest aircraft was the Beverley transport, developed from the General Aircraft Universal Freighter; 47 were built for the RAF, equipping five squadrons between 1956 and 1967. The Beverley performed well in tasks until replaced by the Lockheed Hercules. *M. J. Hooks Collection*

Right:
First flown in 1926, the Boulton Paul Sidestrand medium bomber was remarkably manoeuvrable and an excellent bombing and gunnery platform. Only 18 were built, all serving with No 101 Sqn which eventually converted to the Overstrand.
Dowty Boulton Paul Ltd/M. J. Hooks Collection

biplane day bombers, beginning with the Bristol Jupiter-powered Sidestrand, which entered RAF service in 1928. The next development produced the improved Overstrand, the first RAF bomber to feature a power-operated gun-turret, but the third stage, the Superstrand, remained a project only. Prototypes only were produced of the P31 Bittern and P33 Partridge fighters, the P41 Phoenix, a private two-seater parasol monoplane, and the P64 Mailplane, first flown in March 1933.

Two triple-finned models of the P64 with two Armstrong Siddeley Jaguar VIA radials, designated P71A, were delivered to Imperial Airways in February 1935 for use as light freighters and VIP transports. In 1934, the aviation interests were transferred to a new company, Boulton Paul Aircraft Ltd, and this was followed two years later by a move from Mousehold Aerodrome, Norwich, to new works at Wolverhampton. Wartime success was achieved with the Defiant, a two-seat low-wing monoplane fighter, flown for the first time on 11 August 1937. A total of 1,065 Defiants were built and served from December 1939. After the war, the company built almost 200 Rolls-Royce Merlin-powered P108 Balliol and Sea Balliol advanced two-seat trainers, first flown on 24 March 1948, and the P111 and P120 delta-wing transonic speed research aircraft, which flew on 10 October 1950 and 6 August 1952 respectively, before withdrawing from aircraft manufacture in 1954.

Left:
Developed from and replacing the Sidestrand, the Boulton Paul Overstrand had an improved performance and was the first RAF bomber to have a power-operated enclosed gun turret. Twenty-four were built for Nos 101 and 144 Sqn, serving as bombers from 1935 to 1937 — less than the Sidestrand's service of almost seven years.
*Dowty Boulton Paul Ltd/
M. J. Hooks Collection*

Centre left:
The Boulton Paul Mailplane, first flown in March 1933, exceeded performance specifications in every way but was destroyed in a crash at Martlesham six months later. Experience with it led to production of two modified versions designated P71A for Imperial Airways.
*Dowty Boulton Paul Ltd/
M. J. Hooks Collection*

Below:
The Boulton Paul Defiant was the RAF's first fighter with a four-gun turret, which represented the type's sole armament. With the same Merlin engine as contemporary Hurricanes and Spitfires and weighing almost 30% more, it was no match for day fighters but did well as a night fighter and later a target tug. *IWM*

Above:
Originally conceived as a turboprop trainer, the Boulton Paul Balliol and its rival the Avro Athena eventually turned to the Rolls-Royce Merlin engine. The Balliol won the RAF contract, and 162 were built, including a number for Ceylon.
M. J. Hooks Collection

Right:
Built to assist research into the aerodynamics of delta wings, the Boulton Paul P111 was the company's first jet. Powered by a Rolls-Royce Nene, it flew in late 1951 and was later modified as the P111A — the photo shows the original configuration. It is preserved at the Midland Air Museum at Coventry Airport.
Boulton Paul Aircraft Ltd

Bristol

Founded by Sir George White at Filton, Bristol, on 19 February 1910, the British & Colonial Aeroplane Co, later to become one of the best known names in British aviation, made an undistinguished start, building the French Zodiac biplane. Several Henri Coanda-designed aircraft then followed, but it was the first flight of the Boxkite trainer on 31 July 1910 which signalled the beginning of a turnaround, leading to even greater success during World War 1 with the single-seat Scout and the F2 Fighter. More than 5,100 of the latter were built at Filton and Brislington and remained in first line service with the Royal Flying Corps and Royal Air Force for some 15 years. Although aircraft manufacture went into decline after the end of the war, the Bristol Aeroplane Co, as it became known in 1920, still produced around 2,600 new and reconditioned aircraft in the following 10 years. Few of these, including the Brandon, Brownie, Tourer and Boarhound, proved to be successful, the exception being the Bulldog, which made its first flight in May 1927 and became the

RAF's standard single-seat interceptor until the mid-1930s.

After that came the monoplanes. The Blenheim bomber was followed by the Beaufort, Beaufighter, Buckingham and Brigand during World War 2, while design work was started on the Brabazon, a huge eight-engined commercial airliner which made its flight trials on 4 September 1949, and the Wayfarer/Freighter twin-engined utility aircraft. The former was ahead of its time and never made it into production, but the Freighter was supplied to commercial operators in many parts of the world and also served as a military transport in Australia, Canada, New Zealand and Pakistan. Its most famous postwar airliner, however, was the Type 175 Britannia. Although bedevilled by early teething problems, the four-engined 'Whispering Giant' was a superb aircraft and flew the first turbine-powered transatlantic service in the colours of BOAC on 19 December 1957. But the jet age had already arrived and production ceased after 84 aircraft had been built. Bristol was also engaged in many design studies, especially for high-speed research aircraft and

Above:
The Bristol Boxkite (or Standard Biplane) was a copy of a Henri Farman with more refined fittings. By November 1910, production reached two per week and eight were sold to the Russian Government from a total of 16 built, others going to the British Army and a Belgian pilot. The engine was a 50hp Gnome.

Right:
The best British two-seat fighter of World War 1 was the Bristol F2B, known as the Bristol Fighter. Powered by a Rolls-Royce Falcon engine, it served the RAF into the 1930s and a number were civil registered. One is preserved in flying condition by the Shuttleworth Trust at Old Warden. *Rolls-Royce Ltd/M. J. Hooks Collection*

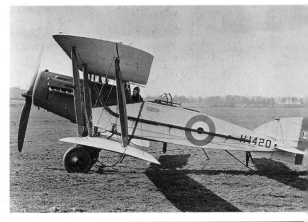

Below:
Well over 4,100 Bristol Blenheims in various versions were built with Bristol Mercury engines of 840 to 920hp. A Blenheim IB was the first British aircraft to cross the German frontier in World War 2. The type was eventually superseded by Douglas Bostons and DH Mosquitoes. Illustrated is a Mk IV bomber. *M. J. Hooks Collection*

Left:
Most widely used RAF fighters in the mid-1930s were the Bristol Bulldogs which served with 10 squadrons. Total production reached 312 fighters plus 59 two-seat trainers. Illustrated is a No 29 Sqn aircraft. *M. J. Hooks Collection*

Below:
Production of the Bristol 170 Freighter in various versions topped 200 and the type served in many countries with civil and military operators. Probably the best known use was as a cross-channel car ferry in the 1950s. Shown is a Mk 31 of Safe Air, New Zealand with its unique passenger pod. *C. H. Parks/Author's Collection*

Above left:
Shown in BEA colours as a potential city centre to city centre airbus, the Bristol 173 helicopter did not go into production but provided valuable data for the Bristol 192 Belvedere — see entry under Westland.

Centre left:
Largest aircraft ever built in Britain, the Bristol Brabazon was intended as a transatlantic airliner. The prototype was powered by eight 2,500hp Bristol Centaurus engines coupled to four sets of contra-rotating propellers. Flown in September 1949, it did not go into production and was scrapped along with two semi-completed airframes in 1953.

Bottom left:
Originally designed as a torpedo bomber, the Bristol Brigand emerged as a light bomber with two 2,470hp Bristol Centaurus engines. Between 1946 and 1950, 143 Brigands were delivered to the RAF, its last piston-engined bomber. They served in the Middle and Far East.

Above:
Known as the 'Whispering Giant', the elegant Bristol Britannia, powered by four 4,400ehp Bristol Siddeley Proteus turboprops, had a protracted development programme but production eventually totalled 84, including 21 for export and 20 for the RAF. Shown is a Series 312 of BOAC. *M. J. Hooks Collection*

supersonic transports, and also built helicopters, including the five-seat Sycamore and the Type 173, Britain's first multi-engined helicopter. The 173 was later developed into the 30-passenger Type 192 and built as the Belvedere by Westland Helicopters, after that company's take-over of Bristol's helicopter interests on 23 March 1960. At the same time, Bristol became part of the newly-established British Aircraft Corporation (BAC) and the name disappeared altogether in December 1963 when it was reorganised as BAC's Filton Division.

British Aerospace (BAe)

Following the passing of the Aircraft and Shipbuilding Industries Act by the British Government, enshrining the nationalisation of the industry, ownership of the British Aircraft Corporation (BAC), Hawker Siddeley Aviation, Hawker Siddeley Dynamics and Scottish Aviation was transferred to a new corporation under the name of British Aerospace (BAe) on 29 April 1977. The original companies retained their identities until the early 1980s when BAe was partially privatised. Full privatisation followed in May 1985. Since its foundation, BAe has undergone numerous internal reorganisation processes, resulting in the closure of its Weybridge, Kingston and Hatfield sites, and the sale of its 125/1000 business jet line to US company Raytheon. The present organisational structure comprises BAe (Commercial Aircraft) Ltd, centred at Woodford, and BAe Defence Ltd at Warton, in Cheshire and Lancashire respectively. Within the commercial aircraft division are: BAe Airbus Ltd, making the wings for all Airbus models at Bristol and Chester; Avro International Aerospace, founded in 1990 to develop the four-engined 146 family of twin-jets into the RJ Series at Woodford; and Jetstream Aircraft Ltd, which produces the Jetstream turboprop aircraft at Prestwick in Scotland. Jetstream Aircraft is joining with Aérospatiale/Alenia to form a new European regional aircraft consortium. BAe Defence Ltd, formed in January 1992, combines the former BAe (Military Aircraft) Ltd with BAe Dynamics.

When BAe was formed, it completed the last few orders of the BAC/Aérospatiale Concorde supersonic airliner and the BAC One-Eleven twinjet. The rights to the latter were sold to Romania in 1979, where Romaero has produced another nine aircraft to date, known as the ROMBAC One-Eleven. BAe also acquired the production lines of the Panavia Tornado; Hawker Siddeley Harrier jump jet, the 50-seat 748 turboprop airliner and 125 business jet; Hawk

39

Below:
The BAe ATP (Advanced Turbo-Prop) was developed from the very successful Avro 748, but has not been as fortunate. Production ceased early in 1995 after around 60 had been built. Several are in service with British Airways and the British Midland Group, while sales have been achieved in Bangladesh, Portugal, Turkey and the USA, the largest operator being United Express carrier Air Wisconsin.

Bottom:
Starting life as the Handley Page Jetstream, the type was taken over by BAe as the Jetstream 31 and has achieved considerable success in the commuter airliner market with around 400 sales, many to the USA.

trainer/light combat aircraft, and relaunched the small Jetstream regional aircraft as the Jetstream 31. As part of a continual updating process, BAe developed the 748 Series 2B, first flown on 22 June 1979, with twin Rolls-Royce Dart RDa7 Mk536-2 turboprops, and the final variant was the Super 748 with a completely new flightdeck and hush-kitted engines. Production of the successful 748 ceased in 1989 after the completion of 379 aircraft, including 31 rear-loading Andover CMk.1s for the RAF and 89 built under licence in India. The larger 64-seat ATP (Advanced Turboprop), designed to succeed the Super 748, has sold only in small numbers and production appears now to have ceased. Several versions of the 125 culminated in the larger, intercontinental-range BAe 125-1000, which made its first flight on 16 June 1990.

The four turbofan-engined BAe146 airliner, produced in a short-body Series 100, stretched Series 200 and even longer Series 300 version for up to 128 passengers, received a new lease of life with the development of the Avroliner RJ family. This differs principally in the adoption of the Textron Lycoming LF507 turbofans in place of the ALF 502s, giving improved performance. Four versions are available: the RJ70, RJ85, RJ100 and RJ115 models.

The 19-seat Jetstream 31, although remaining in production, is now being replaced by the larger 29-seat Jetstream 41, first flown at Prestwick on 25 September 1991.

On the military front, the two-seat Hawk 100 trainer and single-seat Hawk 200 light combat aircraft, both powered by the Rolls-Royce Turbomeca Adour Mk 871 non-afterburning turbofan, are in full production, having replaced earlier RAF and export versions. Deliveries are continuing of the T-45 Goshawk, a naval version for the US Navy, developed jointly with McDonnell Douglas. Tornado production has been extended with the latest order from the Royal Saudi Air Force for 48 Tornado IDS (interdictor strike) models, bringing total production to 992 aircraft, including 795 IDS and 197 ADV (air defence variant). Tornado 2000 is a proposed single-seat successor for low-level, high-speed, long-range missions. Production of the first-generation Harrier continues only in the Sea Harrier variants. BAe also has a stake in Eurofighter 2000, previously known as EFA, an advanced single-seat fighter/ground attack aircraft being developed with Germany, Italy and Spain. The first UK-built prototype made its maiden flight at Warton on 6 April 1994.

Above:
BAe is in the Panavia partnership with Germany and Italy building the Tornado which is in service in the three countries and Saudi Arabia; examples of the latter are shown in the interdictor/strike role.

Overleaf:
The BAe Hawk proved a worthy successor to the Hunter in RAF and export service. While the majority are two-seat 100 series as illustrated, sales have also been made with the 200 single-seater and the type serves, in its two-seat form, with the RAF's Red Arrows aerobatic team.

Above:
Having achieved less commercial success than it deserved, the four-engined 146 regional jet has been developed into the Avroliner RJ series, with better and more reliable Textron Lycoming LF507 turbofans. Four models are being offered, varying in seating capacity from 70–128 seats.

Left:
The Jetstream 41 retained the same fuselage cross-section as the Jetstream 31, but was lengthened to accommodate up to 29 passengers. Other major differences are 1,500hp TPE331-14GR turboprop engines and integral airstairs in the forward door.

Below left:
The delta-canard winged Eurofighter 2000, being developed jointly by the UK, Germany, Italy and Spain, has suffered from political indecision as well as technical problems. It is not now expected to be in service until the year 2000 at the earliest.

Top right:
The Sea Harrier is a maritime version of the Harrier, equipping the Royal Navy. The latest FRS2 development features a Blue Vixen pulse-Doppler radar and AIM-120 advanced medium-range air-to-air missiles. It can also be distinguished from the earlier FRS1 model by its longer rear fuselage and larger nose radome.
M. J. Hooks Collection

British Aircraft Corporation (BAC)

The establishment of the British Aircraft Corporation (BAC) on 1 July 1960 was the result of a desperate need to reorganise and rationalise the aircraft manufacturing industry, following a decade of fragmentation and disarray after World War 2, when a total of 21 airframe and eight aero-engine companies were in existence. Bristol Aircraft, English Electric, Hunting Aircraft and Vickers-Armstrong all became part of BAC, while the other major companies came under the umbrella of Hawker Siddeley. The first aircraft to wear the 'BAC' prefix was the One-Eleven, based on the Hunting H.107 project for a twin-engined short to medium-haul airliner. The Rolls-Royce Spey-powered aircraft made its first flight at Bournemouth–Hurn on 20 August 1963 and went into service with BUA and Braniff in April 1965. By that time, the technically excellent, but commercially unsuccessful, Vanguard four-engined turboprop and four-engined turbofan VC10 airliner had also entered service, while the advanced TSR2 attack and reconnaissance bomber was controversially cancelled, bringing BAC close to collapse.

Below:
Based on the design of the Jet Provost, the BAC Strikemaster was aimed at the export market and achieved considerable success with around 150 built for nine overseas countries. Illustrated is a Mk 88 of the Royal New Zealand Air Force.

An order from BEA for the stretched One-Eleven 500 and the development of the Super VC10 kept things going, as did the former English Electric Lightning, the Jaguar tactical support and training aircraft, developed jointly with France by the SEPECAT consortium, and the BAC 167 Strikemaster, another combat aircraft which was developed from the BAC 145 Jet Provost trainer and flew for the first time on 26 October 1967. Although commercially a disaster, the Anglo-French Concorde supersonic airliner, which took to the skies on 2 March 1969 and flies at more than twice the speed of sound, remains a superb technical and

Below:
Joint development of the Jaguar strike aircraft was undertaken by the Anglo-French SEPECAT consortium comprised of British Aircraft Corporation and Breguet on the airframe, with Rolls-Royce, Turbomeca and SNECMA on the engine. Single-seat tactical strike and two-seat training versions are in service in Britain, France, India and Ecuador.

Bottom:
Many BAC One-Elevens are still in service 32 years after the prototype's first flight. It has been Britain's most successful pure jet airliner with more than 220 built. Nine have been built subsequently in Romania as the ROMBAC One-Eleven.

Above:
Starting life with Vickers, the VC10 eventually came under BAC. With its rear-mounted engines, the VC10 was exceptionally quiet internally, but achieved limited success. Standard and stretched Super versions served with BOAC (30), BUA (three), East African Airways (three), Ghana Airways (three) and the RAF (14). Some airline aircraft were later converted for the RAF as aerial tankers.

Below:
Concorde, built jointly by Aérospatiale and BAC, needs little introduction. The world's only supersonic airliner in service, it recently celebrated 25 years with British Airways and Air France. Thoughts are now turning to a successor. *M. J. Hooks Collection*

collaborative tribute to BAC. On the negative side, projects for large-capacity 200 and 250-seat aircraft (BAC Two-Eleven and Three-Eleven respectively) came to nothing, and an expected participation in the Airbus was scuppered when the Government pulled out in August 1969. Britain eventually rejoined. Studies into variable-geometry technology eventually resulted in the twin-engined, two-seat multi-role Tornado fighter aircraft. First flown in Germany on 14 August 1974, Tornado was conceived as a joint venture between BAC, MBB (Germany) and Fiat (Italy) under the Panavia name. After much merger speculation, which had first surfaced as early as 1967 and had caused a great deal of uncertainty in the years after, BAC was nationalised on 29 April 1977, being joined with Hawker Siddeley Aviation, Hawker Siddeley Dynamics and Scottish Aviation to form British Aerospace (BAe).

Britten-Norman

After John Britten and Desmond Norman finished their apprenticeship at the de Havilland Technical School, they formed a partnership to build aircraft. Setting up operations at Bembridge on the Isle of Wight, their first project was the BN-1F Finibee, an unsuccessful ultra-light monoplane of which only one example was built in 1950. After a period converting and operating agricultural aircraft, Britten-Norman turned its attention back to design, coming up with the BN-2A Islander, a low-cost 10-seat high-wing STOL aircraft for utility and short-haul third-level operations. The prototype made its first flight at Bembridge on 13 June 1965. Originally powered by Lycoming piston engines, the company later added the BN-2T turbine version and a military derivative, known as the Defender. Soon other projects were

Above:
Some 1,200 Islanders have been built in both civil and military versions since its first flight in June 1965. This BNT Defender of the Moroccan Ministry of Fisheries and Merchant Marine is equipped with Omega/GPS, long-range Nav/comms suites and FLIR systems.

Left:
The BN2A MkIII Trislander was a distinctive larger version of the Islander, with capacity for 17 passengers and a third piston engine mounted in a much modified tail unit. A total of 73 were built in the UK, with another 12 in the USA as the Tri-Commutair.

taking shape, including the BN-3 Nymph, which never saw production, and the BN-2A MkIII Trislander, which did. This stretched, three-engined aircraft modelled on the Islander first flew on 11 September 1970.

In spite of the success of the Islander — production was up to 12 aircraft a month at Bembridge and in Romania and the Philippines — the company went into receivership and was acquired by the Fairey Group in August 1972 and renamed Fairey Britten-Norman. A new production line was set up at Fairey's Gosselies factory in Belgium and the 500th Islander was delivered in 1973. Misfortune continued and after Fairey went into liquidation, the company was bought by Pilatus Aircraft of Switzerland, which renamed it Pilatus Britten-Norman on 24 January 1979. Production of the Islander and Defender series continues at Bembridge and at the Romaero works in Bucharest. The latest development is the airborne surveillance Defender 4000, first flown at Bembridge on 17 August 1994. Total production at the end of 1994 amounted to more than 1,200 aircraft.

Carden-Baynes

In 1935, Sir John Carden and L. E. Baynes designed a single-seat powered sailplane, known as the Scud, one example of which was built by Abbots-Baynes Aircraft Ltd at Farnham, Surrey. When the two designers founded the Carden-Baynes Aircraft Ltd at Heston, Middlesex in 1936, they embarked on another project, the ultralight Bee, flown on 3 April 1937. This was a side-by-side two-seater, powered by two 40hp Carden Ford SP1 converted car engines driving pusher propellers. All activities ceased in the 1930s when Heston was requisitioned by the Air Ministry.

Central

The Central Aircraft Co was established in 1916 at Kilburn, North London, as a subsidiary of local joinery firm R. Cattle Ltd, and went on to build a small number of biplanes at its Palmerston Works, all designed by A. A. Fletcher. These were the Centaur IIA, offered as an open cockpit model with accommodation for two pilots and six passengers and an improved cabin version for seven passengers, and the three-seat Centaur IV. Eight Centaur IVs were built and operated by the company's own flying school at Northolt. The postwar slump, however, had a marked effect on the company's activities and it finally closed down in May 1926.

Chilton

The Chilton DW1 is best remembered for the exceptional speed of 112mph, achieved with just a single 32hp Carden Ford water-cooled engine. The

all-wooden, low-wing monoplane was designed and built in 1937 at Chilton, Hungerford, Berkshire, by the Hon Andrew Dalrymple and A. R. Ward, both ex-students at the de Havilland Technical School, operating under the name of the Chilton Aircraft Ltd, which was established in 1936. The availability of the lighter French-built 44hp Train 4T air-cooled engine produced the still faster DW1A, which made its first flight in July 1939. Assembly was also started on another version, the DW2, but the war halted any further work on this and several other types under development. The operation was revived as the Chilton Aircraft Co on 5 June 1946, again at Hungerford, with the intention to achieve certification for the DW1A as the Chelsea Chilton, but these plans came to nothing.

Above:
The diminutive Chilton DW1 achieved a speed of 112mph with a 32hp Carden Ford engine in 1939 and subsequently 126mph with a 44hp French-built Train. Re-engined postwar with a 62hp Walter Mikron, it reached 144.5mph in the 1957 King's Cup race. Four Chiltons were completed; all survived the war and another was built in 1994. *M. J. Hooks Collection*

Below:
Originally built with a single fin and rudder and unconventional control system, the Chrislea Ace was later redesigned with twin fins and rudders as the Super Ace with a 145hp DH Gipsy Major engine. Of the 27 laid down, only 16 were completed and flown. A tail-wheel version, the Skyjeep, accounted for five more, but two were abandoned before completion. Export sales numbered five. *M. J. Hooks Collection*

Chrislea

The first aircraft built by Chrislea Aircraft Co Ltd at Heston was the 1938-vintage LC1 Airguard trainer, designed by R. C. Christophorides. Only one was built before the company went over to component manufacture for military aircraft during the war, but in 1946 construction started of a more successful high-wing monoplane, also designed by Christophorides. The four-seat CH3 Series 1 Ace featured a revolutionary control system, with all control effected by a single wheel mounted on a column. After the closure of Heston in 1947, Chrislea moved to Exeter Airport at Clyst Honiton in Devon, and developed the CH3 Series 2 Super Ace, which differed in having a greater metal content and the more powerful de Havilland Gipsy Major 10 engine. The new control system ran into opposition from potential buyers and production aircraft reverted to a conventional joy-stick and rudder bar control. A total of 16 Super Ace models were built, together with three CH3 Series 4 Skyjeep. This first flew on 21 November 1949 and could be used as a four-seat passenger aircraft or as a freighter and ambulance version with a removable rear fuselage roof covering. The company's assets were acquired by C. E. Harper Aircraft in 1952.

Civilian

The CAC Coupé, built at Hull Municipal Airport, Hedon, East Yorkshire, was the only product of the Civilian Aircraft Co Ltd, established in 1928 by Harold D. Boultbee. A strut-braced, high-wing aircraft, the Coupé was of mixed wood and metal construction and could accommodate two people in a staggered seating arrangement. Two versions were built between 1929 and 1932, the Mk I with a 75hp ABC Hornet flat four engine, and the Mk II, powered by the 100hp Armstrong Siddeley Genet Major I. Total production was one Mk I and five Mk II.

Comper

After designing a number of ultra-light aircraft for the Cranwell Light Aeroplane Club, Flt-Lt Nicholas Comper founded the Comper Aircraft Co Ltd in 1929 and proceeded to build the CLA7 Swift at Hooton Park Aerodrome, Wirral, Cheshire. The Swift was a single-seat sporting aircraft, powered by a 120hp Gipsy III or 130hp Gipsy Major engine, which gained a remarkable reputation among sports flyers. Production was moved to Heston in 1933, where the last of 41 aircraft left the production line that same year. Comper also built the three-seater Mouse,

Above right:
The CAC Coupé II was an improved model, powered by the 100hp Genet Major radial engine, and used in a number of aerial races. The example shown was the last to be built to an order from Germany, where it remained in use until the outbreak of World War 2.
Philip Jarrett Collection

Right:
A popular sports aircraft, the Comper Swift was built with a number of engines from 40 to 130hp; G-ABUU illustrated has a 75hp Pobjoy R. A number were sold abroad, several survived the war in Britain and are still airworthy. *M. J. Hooks Collection*

single-seat Streak racer, and the two-seat Kite tourer at Heston, but in prototype form only. The firm's assets were transferred in June 1934 to a new company named Heston Aircraft Ltd.

Cunliffe-Owen

On 9 August 1937 Sir Hugo Cunliffe-Owen, chairman of British-American Tobaccó, founded BAO at Eastleigh near Southampton. The company changed its name to Cunliffe-Owen Aircraft Ltd in May 1938, and improved and re-engined a single example of the American 14-seat Burnelli UB-14 airliner under the designation OA1, replacing the two Pratt & Whitney radials with Bristol Perseus XIVs. Staying with airliners, W. Garrow-Fisher later designed a medium-range, 10-seat, low-wing transport with twin Alvis Leonides LE 4M engines, named Concordia. The first flight took place at Eastleigh on 19 May 1947, but only two were eventually completed, an extensive sales tour of Europe having failed to win sufficient orders to proceed into series production. Cunliffe-Owen never recovered from this setback and went out of business in 1948.

Dart

A small number of ultra-light aircraft were built by Dart Aircraft Ltd at Dunstable, Bedfordshire, in 1936. The first was the single-seat pusher type Pup, initially referred to as the Dunstable Dart when the company was still known as Zander & Weyl Ltd. The Pup was

followed by the low-wing Kitten, fitted with a 36hp Aeronca-JAP, the J-99 replacing the 27hp Avia 4a-00 flat-four engine, and the tiny Flittermouse. All three were designed by A. R. Weyl.

de Bolotoff

Prince Serge de Bolotoff tried his hand at aircraft design in 1919 with a two-seat general purpose biplane, designated SDEB 14. Only one example, powered by a 200hp Curtiss water-cooled engine, was built at the de Bolotoff Aeroplane Works in Sevenoaks, Kent.

Deekay

The Deekay Knight was an elegant two-seater, designed by S. C. Hart-Still and powered by one 90hp Blackburn Cirrus Minor 1 engine. However, only a single unit was built by the Deekay Aircraft Corporation Ltd at Broxbourne, Hertfordshire, in 1937.

Below:
Cunliffe-Owen at Southampton built the 10-seat Concordia feeder liner with two 550hp Alvis Leonides engines. Flown in 1947, the second prototype undertook an extensive European sales tour and a production batch of six was laid down, but work was suspended in November 1947 as sufficient markets could not be found. *M. J. Hooks Collection*

de Havilland

After the demise of Airco, its chief designer Geoffrey (later Sir Geoffrey) de Havilland was able to form the de Havilland Aircraft Co on 25 September 1920, with some financial support from Airco's founder, George Holt Thomas. Ten days later, he moved into the small airfield at Stag Lane, off the Edgware Road in north-west London, initially providing sales of and support for surplus wartime aircraft, alongside various design activities. In the 40 years that followed, the de Havilland Aircraft Co became without doubt the most prodigious and prolific of Britain's aircraft manufacturers. The first military aircraft were the DH27 Derby day bomber biplane, and the 12-seat

Top:
The single-seat ultra-light Dart Kitten MkII was the second aircraft to be built. It differed from the prototype in having a more powerful 36hp Aeronca-JAP J-99 engine, revised decking and a simpler undercarriage. *Philip Jarrett Collection*

Above:
Deekay Knight. *Philip Jarrett Collection*

DH29 Doncaster long-range research monoplane, the first British monoplane to be fitted with thick section, high lift, cantilever wings. Development of the latter was abandoned in favour of the eight-seat DH34 airliner, which made its first flight on 26 March 1922 and achieved great success with both Daimler Airways and Instone Air Line. Two DH37 touring aircraft were followed by several paper projects, before the first flight, on 25 July 1923, of the DH42 Dormouse high-performance, two-seat, reconnaissance fighter. Only three prototypes were built, however, and the company again turned to the commercial market with the four-passenger DH50 cabin biplane, designed as a replacement for the DH9C making its first flight in August 1923. Powered by a 230hp Siddeley Puma engine, the DH50/50A and 50J models were built at Stag Lane and under licence by Qantas, West Australian Airways and the Larkin Aircraft Supply Co in Australia, SABCA in Belgium, and by Aero in Czechoslovakia. Alan J. Cobham earned his knighthood for his long-distance survey flights in a DH50 to Rangoon, Cape Town and Melbourne between 1924 and 1926.

The two-seater DH51, single-seat DH52 glider and the single-seat DH53 Hummingbird came next and preceded the famous Moth series, which began with the wooden DH60 Moth. First flown by Geoffrey de Havilland himself on 22 February 1922 and powered by a 60hp ADC Cirrus II engine, the economic two-seater revolutionised private flying and nearly 500 were built in the UK alone. Other family members were the DH60G Gipsy Moth with a de Havilland Gipsy engine, DH60M Moth with a welded-steel fuselage, DH60GIII Moth Major, and

Below:
Eleven de Havilland DH34s were built, of which 10 were used commercially and the last delivered to the RAE. One overseas sale was made to Dobrolet, the Russian airline. The aircraft carried nine passengers and two pilots; illustrated is the sixth production DH34 in Instone Air Line service.

Bottom:
The de Havilland DH50 was designed to replace DH9Cs of the DH Hire Service. In addition to 16 built in Britain, 11 were built in Australia, three in Belgium and seven in Czechoslovakia. Illustrated is G-EBFO, used by Sir Alan Cobham for a number of long-distance survey flights. *M. J. Hooks Collection*

Top:
First of a long line of de Havilland Moths was the DH60, produced in large numbers with engines from 85 to 120hp. G-AAUR was one of two coupé cabin floatplanes used by the British Arctic Air Route Expedition in 1930. DH60s were also built in Finland, France, Norway, Canada and Australia and were exported to many other countries. *M. J. Hooks Collection*

Above:
Built for Imperial Airways' desert airmail service, the DH66 Hercules had three 420hp Bristol Jupiter engines. Up to seven passengers could be carried plus two pilots and a wireless operator. Services began in late December 1926, and 11 were built, four going to West Australian Airways. *M. J. Hooks Collection*

Above:
Best known of all Moths was the DH82 Tiger Moth, and a number are still flying in many parts of the world. Many pilots trained on and made their first solos in Tigers. Few were operated on floats, but S1675 was one of two supplied to the Air Ministry with Short-built floats. *M. J. Hooks Collection*

Below:
This de Havilland DH83 Fox Moth was the first aircraft owned by Max Ward in Canada, operating as Polaris Charter Co Ltd. Ward later developed his business into the famous airline Wardair.

the military DH60T Moth Trainer. The seven-passenger DH66 Hercules, powered by three 420hp Bristol Jupiter VI engines, was a large commercial biplane constructed for Imperial Airways' desert airmail service between Cairo and Karachi. It was first flown on 30 September 1926 and followed by the DH61 Giant Moth, a six/eight-seat airliner, designed in 1927 to an Australian requirement for a DH50J replacement, and the four-seat DH75 Hawk Moth. Further improvements to the Moths resulted in the more comfortable, long-range DH80A Puss Moth with an inverted Gipsy III engine, first flown on 9 September 1929, and the famous DH82A Tiger Moth, which first flew on 26 October 1931. More than 4,200 Tiger Moths were built in the UK, with another 3,000 constructed under licence overseas. The

final aircraft to bear the Moth name were the DH83 Fox Moth, the DH85 Leopard Moth, the DH87 Hornet Moth and the DH94 Moth Minor.

The DH84 Dragon was a twin-engined development of the Fox Moth for six passengers, most of the 115 produced in the UK being used in airline service. This led to several more airliner types, all built at Hatfield Aerodrome, Hertfordshire, including the 10-passenger four Gipsy VI-powered DH86 first flown on 14 January 1934, followed in quick succession by a twin-engined derivative, known as the DH89 Dragon Rapide (728 built), and the smaller DH90 Dragonfly for four passengers. Seven four-engined DH91 Albatross low-wing intercontinental transports for 22 passengers entered airline service in early 1939, as did the smaller, 18-passenger

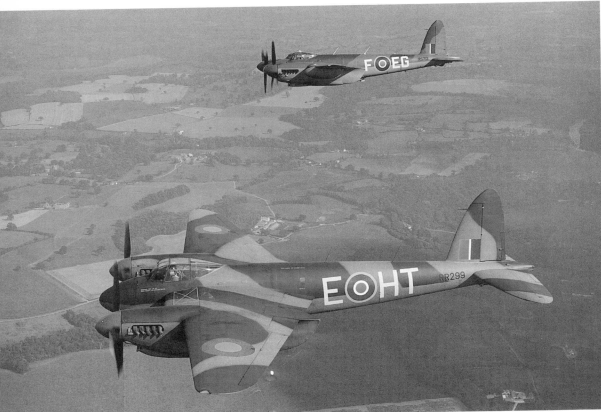

Top:
Beauty of line was a feature of the DH91 Albatross all-wood airliner. With four 525hp DH Gipsy XII engines it had a 3,000+ mile range as a mailplane or 1,000+ miles as a 22-passenger plus four crew airliner, with a maximum speed of more than 220mph. G-AEVV was the prototype, followed by a second and then five production aircraft; all were delivered to Imperial Airways. *M. J. Hooks Collection*

Above:
Wooden construction used in the DH91 provided valuable experience for the DH98 Mosquito, built as a private venture by de Havilland and capable of outpacing contemporary fighters. Its success and versatility are legendary; few survive, but Mosquito T.3 RR299 still flies in the ownership of British Aerospace.

high-wing DH95 Flamingo twin. Mention must also be made of the fast 237mph DH88 Comet, designed specially for the England–Australia air race. The RAF took delivery of 30 DH93 Don three-seat trainers, followed by the immortal DH98 Mosquito, which first flew on 25 November 1940. Many variants were built of this versatile wooden twin-engined World War 2 bomber, fighter and reconnaissance aircraft in the UK, Canada and Australia. A total of 7,781 had been built when production ended in November 1950. Two other types flown before the end of the war and put into large-scale production were the Rolls-Royce Goblin turbojet-powered, twin-boom DH100 Vampire and the twin-engined DH103 Hornet, a scaled-down version of the Mosquito, and its naval equivalent, the Sea Hornet. The Vampire was later developed into the DH112 Venom and Sea Venom two-seat all-weather fighters in 1949, and into the DH115 Vampire Trainer. Another two-seat all-weather naval fighter was the DH110 Sea Vixen, which entered service with the Royal Navy in June 1957.

De Havilland's first postwar civil product was the twin Gipsy-powered DH104 Dove, large numbers of which were built at Hatfield and at Hawarden Aerodrome, Chester. The prototype first flew on 25 September 1945 and production aircraft appeared in many civil variants, as well as in military configurations as the Devon C Mk1 and Sea Devon Mk 20. The four-engined 14–17 passenger DH114 Heron airliner, which first flew on 10 May 1950, used many Dove components. Pride of place among postwar civil airliners, however, must go to the DH106 Comet, the world's first jet transport to enter revenue service. Powered by four 4,450lb st Rolls-Royce Ghost turbojets buried in the wing roots, the prototype of the 36-44 seat Comet I flew for the first time on 27 July 1949 and operated the first passenger service on 2 May 1952, drastically cutting journey times. After three disastrous structural inflight failures the type was withdrawn, but the later Comet 4/4B/4C models, all powered by four 10,500lb st Rolls-Royce Avons and seating up to 78 passengers, operated successfully in many parts of the world. Total production amounted to 112, including 74 Series 4 aircraft. Design work was started in the late 1950s on the DH121 Trident and the DH125 executive jet, but these were developed and constructed by Hawker Siddeley after the take-over of de Havilland in 1960.

Right:
The de Havilland Vampire Trainer was developed as a private venture and flew in November 1950. Adopted as the standard RAF advanced trainer and designated Vampire T.11, 804 were built including many T.55 export models for more than 20 countries. Manufacture was also undertaken in India and Australia. Shown is the first of six T.55s for the Iraqi Air Force. *M. J. Hooks Collection*

Above:
Basically a scaled-up Dove, the DH114 Heron received its CofA on 20 November 1950. Pictured are two 15-seat Herons in service with Sky of Siam, used both on passenger services and on artificial rain-making flights with a hopper attached to the underside of the fuselage.

Below:
The Edgley Optica observation aircraft flew in December 1979 with a 180hp Avco-Lycoming piston engine driving a ducted fan; later models had an uprated engine. It had a chequered career, ownership of the design passing through several companies, although a number were built. *M. J. Hooks Collection*

Below:
English Electric built two Wren ultra-light aircraft powered by 398cc ABC motorcycle engines for the *Daily Mail* Light Aeroplane Competition at Lympne in October 1923. One shared prizes with an ANEC monoplane, achieving fuel consumption of 87.5 miles/gallon. A Wren is maintained in airworthy condition by the Shuttleworth Trust. *M. J. Hooks Collection*

Bottom:
Britain's first jet bomber was the English Electric Canberra. The type might be described as the Mosquito of the jet age, representing considerable advances over the types it replaced. It was produced in many variants, including the Martin B-57 series built in USA, and was sold to many countries, also serving the RAF for over 40 years; WJ764 was a B Mk 6. *M. J. Hooks Collection*

Edgley

Edgley Aircraft Ltd was formed in 1974 at Old Sarum Airfield, Salisbury, Wiltshire to build a specialised observation aircraft, the three-seat EA7 Optica, designed by John Edgley for exceptional all-round view, slow speed and quiet performance. Powered by a single ducted propulsor unit with a 260hp Avco-Lycoming flat-six engine, it first flew on 14 December 1979 and gained CAA certification in February 1985. In spite of a large number of orders, financial difficulties forced Edgley Aircraft into receivership and a new company, Optica Industries Ltd, restarted production in January 1986. But bad luck continued to dog the aircraft and many were destroyed in a severe hangar fire on 16 January 1987. Renamed Brooklands Aircraft Co Ltd on 14 April 1987, the company then offered two versions with differing avionics packages, the Optica Scout I and II, and projected an electronic surveillance derivative known as the Scoutmaster. The company failed again

in March 1990 and was bought by FLS Lovaux, which took over Optica production, but is itself now looking for a buyer.

English Electric

The English Electric Co was founded in 1918 by Phoenix Dynamo (Bradford), Dick, Kerr (Preston) and Coventry Ordnance Works (COW), all of which had built aircraft under subcontract during the war, and two other non-aviation companies. Early products included the Cork, Ayr and Kingston flying boats, followed by the Wren single-seat ultralight designed by W. O. Manning for the Lympne Trials of October 1923. A depressed business environment forced the closure of the aviation department in 1926, but as war drew closer, the company won a big order for subcontract work and built several thousand aircraft from 1938 and through the war years. These included Handley Page Hampden and Halifax bombers and the de Havilland Vampire fighter, built at the former Dick, Kerr works at Strand Road, Preston, Lancashire.

After the war, the company decided to stay in aircraft production and designed Britain's first turbojet bomber, the Canberra, which flew for the first time on 13 May 1949 and served in many different versions with the RAF and air forces across the world. A total of 631 Rolls-Royce Avon-powered Canberras were built by English Electric, with another 194 by Avro, Handley Page and Shorts. An additional 48 were built in Australia and 403 more in the USA by the Martin company as the B-57 with Pratt & Whitney turbofans.

W. E. W. Petter, who led the design of the Canberra, then produced an advanced single-seat supersonic fighter prototype, known as the P1A,

which exceeded the speed of sound during its first flight on 4 August 1954. Three more prototypes followed under the designation of P1B and were developed into the famous Lightning interceptor, which entered RAF service in December 1959. English Electric also won a development contract, jointly with Vickers, for a Tactical Strike Reconnaissance aircraft, the TSR2, which was based largely on the P17A design of Freddie (later Sir Freddie) Page, who had taken over at Warton from Teddy Petter. At the beginning of the year, on 9 January 1959, the company was reorganised as English Electric Aviation Ltd, but became part of the British Aircraft Corporation on 1 January 1960. Continuing production of the Lightning at the BAC Preston Division, the original name finally disappeared on 1 January 1964 and the axe also fell on the TSR2.

Fairey

From building excellent flying models, electrical engineer C. R. (later Sir Richard) Fairey and his company Fairey Aviation Co Ltd, formed on 15 July 1915, came to prominence with a series of good

Below:
The English Electric Lightning was the RAF's first fighter to exceed Mach 1 in level flight and entered service in December 1959. Two Rolls-Royce Avons gave a total 22,500lb thrust (28,860lb with reheat) and a maximum speed off M.2+. Several versions were built in the total production of 340 including 40 for Saudi Arabia and 14 for Kuwait.

Right:
Designed for reconnaissance and general purposes, Fairey IIIF production reached 662 including prototypes and export versions. It was the last of a long line of Fairey III series variants of which almost 1,000 were built and served with the RAF and Royal Navy with Napier Lion engines. Some were re-engined with the Armstrong Siddeley Panther radial engine and became Gordons. *M. J. Hooks Collection*

military aircraft, mostly for naval service. Initially assembling the Short 827 at its factory in Clayton Road, Hayes, Middlesex, Fairey soon embarked on its own designs, among early examples being the Campania two-seat patrol seaplane, the Hamble Baby single-seat anti-submarine seaplane and landplane trainers featuring variable-camber flaps, and the Fairey III reconnaissance biplanes, of which almost 1,000 were built in several different versions between 1917 and 1930. Next came the Flycatcher single-seat fighter and the Fawn light bomber and reconnaissance aircraft, developed from the Pintail and flown in March 1923, but its ungainly appearance and poor performance soon gave way to the fast Fox day bomber, powered by a 480hp Curtiss D-12 engine. The Gordon medium-range day bomber was similar to the Fairey IIIF, the main difference being the 525hp Armstrong Siddeley Panther IIA radial air-cooled engine in place of the Napier Lion water-

Top:
Probably the most famous Fairey aircraft was the Swordfish which entered service in 1936 and served throughout the war with the Royal Navy. Outliving its intended replacement, the Fairey Albacore, its exploits were legendary. Several of the 2,391 built survive, including two airworthy examples with the Royal Navy Historic Flight, one of which is shown.

Above:
The two-seat Fairey Fulmar was the Royal Navy's first purpose-designed monoplane fighter and the last of 600 was delivered in February 1943. It saw action for the first time in 1940 defending Malta convoys and was a useful stop-gap before the arrival of a single-seaters such as the Seafire. *M. J. Hooks Collection*

cooled engine. The Seal was the Fleet Air Arm version. Another aircraft of note was the Hendon heavy night-bomber, which first flew in November 1930 and served with the RAF from 1937 to 1939. Most of these were built at new larger premises at Hyde Road, Hayes and other works at Stockport, Cheshire and Hamble Aerodrome in Hampshire. In 1930, Fairey opened Great West Aerodrome at Harmondsworth, Middlesex, which after 1945 was converted into London Heathrow Airport.

Major World War 2 types were the magnificent and versatile Swordfish naval aircraft (2,391 built), developed from the TSRII (Torpedo-Spotter-Reconnaissance) which flew on 17 April 1934; the Battle land-based light monoplane bomber, flown on 10 March 1936; the Barracuda, the first monoplane torpedo-bomber to enter service with the Royal Navy; the Albacore torpedo-bombing biplane, first flown on 12 December 1938 and originally intended as a Swordfish replacement; and the Rolls-Royce Merlin-powered Fulmar two-seat Fleet fighter. The two-seat Firefly reconnaissance fighter saw active service towards the end of the war. When peace returned, the company experimented with helicopters which incorporated a number of new design principles. These included the four-seat Gyrodyne with a conventional propeller replacing the usual anti-torque rotor; the Jet Gyrodyne with a tip-jet rotor drive converted from the Gyrodyne, and the large 40-passenger Rotodyne. Fairey also built two delta-wing jet research aircraft, the FD1 and FD2. The latter, powered by the Rolls-Royce Avon RA5, became the world's first aircraft to exceed 1,000mph, on 10 March 1956. The only postwar fixed-wing type to go into full-scale production was the Gannet naval fighter which entered service with the Fleet Air Arm in 1955. Later versions were completed by Westland Aircraft Ltd, following its take-over of Fairey in May 1960.

Below:
Designed as a torpedo/dive-bomber, the Fairey Barracuda was intended to replace the Albacore biplane. Its strange appearance, with folding wings, a stalky undercarriage, large flaps and high-set braced tailplane, was dictated by naval requirements. A total of 2,602 were built between 1939 and 1947 by several companies. Illustrated is a Fairey-built Mk 1.
M. J. Hooks Collection

Right:
The Fairey Firefly was used as a fighter, reconnaissance, anti-submarine and trainer aircraft, with later conversions to the unmanned aerial target role and target tug. Total production reached 1,570 including 54 for the Royal Netherlands Naval Air Service. Other overseas customers included Canada, Australia, Denmark, Ethiopia, Sweden, India and Thailand. Shown is one of five Indian Navy target-tugs.
M. J. Hooks Collection

Below right:
A Fairey Gannet made the first deck landing by a propeller-turbine aircraft aboard HMS *Illustrious* on 19 June 1950. Using an Armstrong Siddeley Double-Mamba engine — two engines coupled to contra-rotating propellers — the Gannet was a search and strike aircraft and 349 were built in five versions including trainers. Export models went to Indonesia, Australia and West Germany. Illustrated is a Royal Navy Gannet AEW.3 early warning variant.

Above:
The Fairey Rotodyne was a bold attempt to provide a vertical take-off airliner for city centre to city centre operations. Powered by two Napier Eland turboprops for forward flight and pressure jet units at the rotor blade tips, it was extensively tested and attracted considerable interest but was not put into production.
M. J. Hooks Collection

Below:
The Fairey Delta 2 supersonic research aircraft was the company's last fixed-wing type and raised the world's air speed record to 1,132mph, 310mph above the previous record set by a US Super Sabre. It was the first British aircraft to exceed 1,000mph and provided valuable data for the Concorde programme, the second of the two being fitted with an ogival wing in which form it became the BAC.221.
M. J. Hooks Collection

Above:
Designed as a lightweight fighter, the Folland Gnat was more widely used as a two-seat trainer and 105 were supplied to the RAF whose aerobatic team, The Red Arrows, used them until re-equipped with Hawks. Single-seat Gnats were exported to Finland and India, and licence-production in the latter was undertaken by Hindustan Aeronautics as the Ajeet. An early production Finnish Gnat is shown. *M. J. Hooks Collection*

Below:
Geoffrey Wikner's attempt to build a cheaper two-seat light aircraft emerged as the Wicko. This is further described in the text. Eleven were completed, production models having a 90hp Cirrus Minor engine and were priced at £650. G-AFJB was built for the Midland Aero Club; this and six others were impressed during the war but 'JB and one other survived. *M. J. Hooks Collection*

Folland

The year 1935 saw the formation at Hamble, near Southampton, of British Marine Aircraft Ltd, reorganised in May 1937 as Folland Aircraft Ltd, with Harry P. Folland, formerly chief designer of the Gloster Aircraft Co Ltd, as head of the new company. After limiting its activities to major subcontract work during the war and building the 43/37 engine testbed monoplane, Folland began work on a lightweight fighter, the Fo 139 Midge, first flown on 11 August 1954 and designed by W. E. W. Petter, which was eventually developed into the single-seat Fo 141 Gnat. The Bristol Siddeley Orpheus turbojet-powered Gnat first flew in prototype form on 18 July 1955 and went on to much acclaim with the Red Arrows aerial display team. The Gnat T1 with a tandem cockpit made its début on 31 August 1959, just before production was transferred to Hawker Siddeley Aviation, after that company's acquisition of Folland in 1960. A total of 105 were built in the UK between 1959 and 1965, and another 213 under licence by Hindustan Aeronautics Ltd in India, which also developed the Gnat into the Ajeet ground-attack fighter.

Foster Wikner

Cheap and efficient aircraft were the hallmark of Australian aircraft designer Geoffrey N. Wikner, who achieved a measure of success in his own country with his Wicko and Wicko Lion sports monoplanes, before setting up in Britain. Joining with V. Foster and J. F. Lusty, he formed the Foster Wikner

Aircraft Co Ltd, operating from Lusty's furniture factory at Bromley-by-Bow, East London. The first prototype two-seat Wicko FW1, with a modified Ford V8 engine known as the Wicko F, was completed in September 1936, but was later re-engined with a 90hp Cirrus Minor I as the FW2. A 150hp Cirrus Major installation, specifically for the 1937 King's Cup race, resulted in the FW3, and this engine became the standard powerplant for all GM1 production models. The company was by then established at Southampton Airport, Eastleigh, but ceased production at the outbreak of war.

General

Following the closure of Beardmore's aviation interests, H. J. Stieger, a Swiss-born engineer, developed the Monospar system of construction, offering a better strength/weight ratio through the adoption of a Warren girder type assembly. Operating as the Monospar Wing Co Ltd at Croydon, he successfully demonstrated the three-seat Monospar ST-1, built by Gloster Aircraft Co Ltd, and this led to the formation of a new company, General Aircraft Ltd, which began building the four-seat Monospar ST-4 cantilever monoplane at Croydon in 1931. The improved ST-6, with a manually-operated retractable undercarriage, followed in 1933, and in the same year, the company moved into bigger premises at London Air Park, Hanworth in Middlesex. The year 1935 saw the introduction, via the ST-10, ST-11 and ST-12, of the ST-25 Jubilee, so designated and named to celebrate the Silver Jubilee of King George V. This model had an additional folding seat and was also produced in a twin-fin version known as the ST-25 Universal. The 10-seat ST-18 Croydon also made its début in 1935.

Above:
General Aircraft's first production Monospar was the ST-4, a four-seater with two 85hp Pobjoy engines. Flown in May 1932, it led a total production run of 36 before manufacture switched to the improved ST-6.
M. J. Hooks Collection

Left:
Last version of the General Aircraft Monospar was the ST-25, a four-seater with occasional fifth seat, in three variants, Jubilee, De Luxe and Universal. Powered by two 90 or 95hp Pobjoy Niagara engines, 57 were built before production ceased in 1939. G-AEDY was the prototype De Luxe

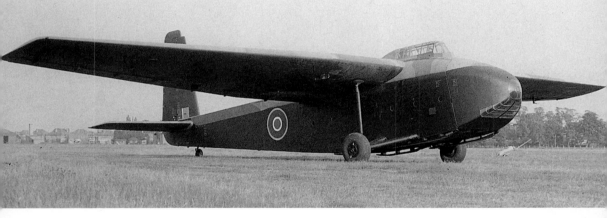

During the war, the company built some smaller aircraft and gliders, including the GAL38 Fleet Shadower, GAL42 Cygnet/GAL45 Owlet two-seat trainer (acquired from bankrupt CW Aircraft Ltd, founded in 1935 by C. R. Chronander and J. I. Waddington), GAL47 twin-boom Air Observation Post, GAL48 Hotspur training glider and the GAL49/58 Hamilcar heavy transport glider and powered freighter, 390 of which were built following the first flight on 27 March 1942. The Cygnet had the distinction of being the first light all-metal, stressed-skin civil aircraft to be produced in the UK. General Aircraft then designed the GAL60 Universal Freighter, a medium-range transport which became the Blackburn Beverley, after General Aircraft merged with Blackburn Aircraft in January 1949.

Top:
The General Aircraft Hotspur was the RAF's standard training glider of World War 2 and over 1,000 were built, many by furniture manufacturer Harris Lebus. Although not used operationally, the Hotspur could carry seven troops.

Above:
The Allies' largest and heaviest glider in World War 2 was the General Aircraft Hamilcar which could carry a seven-ton tank. Towed by Halifaxes and Stirlings, they were used in the D-Day landings in Normandy. Twenty examples of a version with two Bristol Mercury engines were built for use in the Pacific theatre but VJ-Day made this unnecessary. *M. J. Hooks Collection*

Gloster

The Gloucestershire Aircraft Co was formed on 5 June 1917 by Airco and H. H. Martyn at Sunningend Works, Cheltenham. The simpler marketing name of Gloster was adopted in 1926. By the end of 1918, the company had built large numbers of FE2bs, Bristol Fighters and Nieuport Nighthawks, but suffered a considerable downturn after the war when contracts were slashed. After Holt Thomas sold Airco in 1920, the company took over large quantities of Nighthawk parts, which H. P. Folland developed into the Bear and Camel (or Bamel) racers, and the single-seat Sparrowhawk fighter. Folland then designed some of the best known radial-engined

biplane fighters during the interwar years, starting with the high-speed and highly manoeuvrable two-seat Grebe, with which the RAF started to re-equip in 1923. The Grebe was followed into service in 1926 by the improved Gamecock with a 425hp Bristol Jupiter VI engine, and later by the high-performance Gauntlet, superseded in 1937 by the legendary Gladiator and Sea Gladiator, powered by the 840hp Bristol Mercury. In February 1928, Gloster had also flown the Gambet, a single-seat carrier-borne fighter, which was built under licence in Japan for the Imperial Navy.

After Hawker took control of Gloster in May 1934 and the company became part of the Hawker Siddeley Aviation Group the following year, Folland left to

Left:
Between 1923 and 1927, 133 Gloster Grebes were built, the majority being single-seat fighters with two-seat trainers also being constructed. Production Grebe IIs had a 400hp Armstrong Siddeley Jaguar engine giving a top speed of 162mph. Three Grebes went to the Royal New Zealand Air Force. Illustrated is Gloster's demonstrator, G-EBHA, which was fitted with a 455hp Bristol Jupiter engine. *M. J. Hooks Collection*

Bottom left:
The last of Britain's biplane fighters was the Gloster Gladiator, which was fitted with a 840hp Bristol Mercury engine. The prototype, illustrated, used a modified Gauntlet fuselage — note the spatted tailwheel. Total production, including 98 Sea Gladiators, reached 747. More than 300 were in use in 13 countries.

Above:
Britain's first operational jet fighter was the Gloster Meteor which entered service with No 616 Sqn in July 1944. Production aircraft had Rolls-Royce Derwent turbojets and well over 3,500 Meteors of various marks were built by Gloster and Armstrong Whitworth, with a further 330 by Fokker in The Netherlands and Fairey in Belgium. Shown is one of seven ex-RAF Meteors delivered to Israel. *M. J. Hooks Collection*

Below:
The Gloster Javelin all-weather fighter's main characteristic was its large delta wing. First squadron to be re-equipped, replacing Meteor NF.14s, was No 46 at Odiham in February 1946. Seven prototype and 295 production Javelins were built covering nine different marks. This line-up of FAW.9s shows aircraft of Singapore-based No 60 Sqn. *M. J. Hooks Collection*

Above:
Only three examples of the GWE6 Bantam were built at Hendon in 1919. Designed by M. Boudot, this single-seat sporting biplane was powered by one 80hp Le Rhone engine and raced in the 1919 Aerial Derby at Hendon. *Philip Jarrett Collection*

start his own company. Gloster started building several thousand Hawker aircraft, as well as 600 Armstrong Whitworth AW41 Albemarles, assembled by the fictitious A. W. Hawksley. From 1943 onwards, Gloster also designed and built nearly 2,500 Meteors, Britain's first jet-powered combat aircraft. Another 1,067 were assembled by Armstrong Whitworth. The last Gloster aircraft was the massive Javelin night fighter, the first twin-engined delta-wing aircraft, and the first to be designed from the outset as an all-weather fighter. It made its maiden flight on 26 November 1951 and entered RAF service in 1956. A total of 430 were produced in nine different versions by both Gloster and Armstrong Whitworth. In October 1961, the two firms became the Whitworth Gloster Division of Hawker Siddeley, both firms losing their identity on 1 April 1965.

Grahame-White

Claude Grahame-White learnt to fly in 1909 and gained fame as a showman, before developing Hendon Aerodrome and building a succession of aircraft, mostly biplanes, between 1911 and 1919 under the title of The Grahame-White Aviation Co Ltd. As agent for the US Burgess aircraft and later for Morane-Saulnier, Grahame-White redeveloped the Burgess Baby biplane into the New Baby and produced Morane-Saulnier monoplanes for the War Office. Its own product line included the five-seat pusher Type X Aerobus; the Type XI two-seat military biplane and the float-equipped Type XIII, both powered by the 100hp Gnome Monosoupape engine;

the Type XV two-seat biplane trainer in widespread use by the Royal Flying Corps and Royal Naval Air Service during the early part of World War 1; and the unusual twin-fuselage, three-engined GWE4 Ganymede bomber of 1918, converted for civil use as the GWE9 Ganymede. Other civil models were the GWE6 Bantam single-seat sporting biplane and the GWE7, a luxury folding wing transport aircraft for four passengers seated in a glazed compartment.

Handley Page

Frederick (later Sir Frederick) Handley Page first experimented with and built several biplanes and monoplanes at premises in Woolwich, Fambridge and Barking Creek, before settling on works at Cricklewood in north London and Radlett Aerodrome, Hertfordshire. His company, Handley Page Ltd, became the first public company to build aircraft when it was founded on 17 June 1909. Few of his early projects were memorable, in spite of unusual names like Bluebird, Antiseptic and Yellow Peril, until he embarked on the 0/100 in 1911, then the largest aircraft built in Britain. Used primarily as a

Above:
Handley Page 0/10s were among several variants of converted wartime 0/400 bombers operating services in 1919/20. Following three freight conversions came nine for 12 passengers, used between Croydon and the Continent. Usually powered by Rolls-Royce Eagle engines, G-EATK was converted to Bristol Jupiter radials.

Below:
In its passenger configuration, the Handley Page W10 could carry 16, but eventually G-EBMR was converted to a flying tanker for Sir Alan Cobham's non-stop flight to India in Airspeed Courier G-ABXN shown here.
M. J. Hooks Collection

Top:
Best known of the Handley Page airliners between the
wars was the stately HP42. Eight were built for
Imperial Airways' European and Eastern routes,
earning an enviable reputation for reliability and safety
— no passenger was killed up to the outbreak of war
when the HP42 fleet had achieved a mileage of 2.3
million.

Above:
The Handley Page Halifax was Britain's second four-
engine bomber to enter service with the RAF in World
War 2. First versions were powered by Rolls-Royce
Merlin engines but the majority of the 6,176 built had
Bristol Hercules radials. Postwar disposals bred a
number of civil conversions including 12-passenger
Haltons for BOAC. A number of smaller companies
operated converted Halifaxes including the Lancashire
Aircraft Corporation whose G-AKEC flew in the *Daily
Express* Air Race in 1950. It came 24th!

heavy night bomber, the 0/100 featured folding
wings, an enclosed cabin with bullet-proof glass and
armour protection, and engines mounted in armoured
nacelles. Improvements to the 0/100 resulted in the
0/400, powered by twin 360hp Rolls-Royce Eagle
VIII engines, of which more than 450 were built in
the UK in 1918/19. Some of these made useful
interim 10-seat civil transports after the Armistice.
The 0/400 conversion led to the construction of the
company's first purely civil transports, the W8, W9
and W10. Featuring an open cockpit for the pilot and
an enclosed cabin for 15 passengers, the W8 made its
first flight on 4 December 1919, followed on
1 October 1925 by the three-engined W9 (only one
built), and the W10, reverting to two engines, that
same year.

Imperial Airways' requirement for a larger aircraft
for specific sections of the Empire Route was met

with the HP42, an all-metal biplane with the first enclosed cockpit and accommodation for up to 24 passengers. First flown in November 1930, the HP42 served until the advent of war, when the company's production reverted entirely to military bombers. These included the four-engined Halifax and Hampden, along with the Hereford, Harrow and Heyford twin bombers. The twin-engined Hyderabad and Hinaidi night bombers had already entered RAF service in the early 1930s. Long before the war ended, several transport designs were on the drawing board, including the Hastings, first flown on 25 April 1947 with four 1,675hp Bristol Hercules engines and capable of carrying 50 fully-equipped troops, and the four-engined Hermes, the first modern British airliner after the war, which made its first flight on 3 December 1945. Twenty-five of the improved Hermes IV entered service with BOAC in

Top:
First of Britain's postwar large airliners with a tricycle undercarriage, the Handley Page Hermes 4 was preceded by a Mk 2 prototype with a tailwheel. Twenty-five Mk 4s were supplied to BOAC as 65-seaters plus seven crew; a number were later used by charter operators. *M. J. Hooks Collection*

Above:
Originally developed by Miles, the Marathon became a Handley Page responsibility when that company bought Miles in 1948, at which time only two Marathons had been built — the prototype is shown. The type had a chequered history and only 40 were built, 28 of which ultimately went to the RAF as navigation trainers. *M. J. Hooks Collection*

Top:
Conceived as a four piston-engined airliner, in which
form the two prototypes flew, the Handley Page Herald
entered production powered by two Rolls-Royce Dart
turboprops. Forty-eight production Heralds were built,
serving in a number of countries and a few are still
flying. G-BAZJ is shown in Air UK colours.
M. J. Hooks Collection

Above:
Third of the RAF V-bombers to enter service, in
November 1957, was the crescent-winged Handley
Page Victor. As earlier versions were replaced with
Mk 2s, they were converted to flying tankers. XH590,
refuelling a Buccaneer and Sea Vixen, was a Mk K1A.
Eighty-four production Victors were built, and the last,
Mk 2 tankers, were retired in 1994.
M. J. Hooks Collection

August 1950. In the interim, converted Halifax bombers, some later known as the HP70 Halton 1, were pressed into service with BOAC and other airlines. Handley Page also took over production of the Miles Marathon at Woodley Aerodrome, Reading, Berkshire, under the HPR1 Marathon designation, setting up a separate organisation, Handley Page (Reading) Ltd on 5 July 1948. In subsequent years, Handley Page built a number of research aircraft to investigate supersonic flight, new wing shapes and tail-less configurations, some of which were incorporated in the Victor bomber, test flown for the first time on 24 December 1952. This long-range, four-engined bomber, the last of three V-bombers to enter RAF service, had an unusual 'crescent' wing, hydraulically-operated air brakes and a braking parachute in the tail cone. A total of 50 high-wing, short-haul HPR7 Dart Herald airliners were built between 1959 and 1968, and the smaller 18-seat HP137 Jetstream was also put into large-scale production at Radlett. But the high cost of developing this aircraft forced Handley Page into voluntary liquidation on 8 August 1969, and, on 1 June 1970, one of Britain's best-known aircraft manufacturers ceased to exist. The Jetstream was later redeveloped by British Aerospace into a successful regional aircraft.

Below:
The Hawker Hart became the RAF's standard light day bomber in January 1930 and some 1,000 Harts and variants were built in British factories with a further 42 under licence in Sweden. Shown is a one-off non-standard Hart which tested the Rolls-Royce Kestrel V engine with steam cooling and had an enclosed cockpit.

Hawker

On 15 November 1920, the directors of the defunct Sopwith Aviation & Engineering Co Ltd — including Sopwith himself and test pilot Harry G. Hawker, who unfortunately died in flight a few months later, — formed H. G. Hawker Engineering Co Ltd, initially building cars, motorcycles and aircraft spares at its factory at Canbury Park Road, Kingston. First aircraft to be built by the new company were the parasol-wing Duiker reconnaissance monoplane, the Woodcock night fighter and trainer biplane, the Hedgehog two-seat reconnaissance biplane, the Heron single-seat fighter, the Horsley torpedo bomber, and the Cygnet ultralight designed by Sydney Camm, who became chief designer in 1925. Camm then designed the Hart two-seat day bomber biplane, which first flew in June 1928 with a new Rolls-Royce FXI engine and was built in the greatest numbers (2,506), more variants and by more companies than any other British aircraft built between the wars. A civil version with the Rolls-Royce Kestrel IB engine, known as the Hart II, was first flown on 15 September 1932. The basic Hart was adapted for many different roles, producing the Audax army co-operation biplane, Demon two-seat fighter, Hardy and Hartbees general-purpose two-seaters, the Osprey naval fighter-reconnaissance aircraft, the Hind light bomber and its derivative, the Hector army co-operation two-seater. The Hornet single-seat fighter of 1929 led to the Fury, at 245mph the fastest biplane to enter RAF service, and the carrier-based Nimrod. Between 1929 and 1931, Hawker also built 36 Tomtit trainers.

The success of the company led to the formation of Hawker Aircraft Ltd on 18 May 1933, the purchase of Gloster in June 1934 and the establishment of Hawker Siddeley Aircraft Co Ltd, a much larger group whose

members, apart from Hawker and Gloster, included Sir W. G. Armstrong Whitworth Aircraft, Armstrong Siddeley Motors, Air Service Training and A. V. Roe. On 6 November 1936 an aircraft made its maiden flight which was to carve itself a special niche in the annals of the RAF. This was the Hurricane which shared the bulk of Britain's air defence with the Supermarine Spitfire during the Battle of Britain. More than 14,000 of the Rolls-Royce Merlin-powered fighter were built over the next eight years, including approximately 800 Sea Hurricanes. Other military designs included the related Henley light bomber, the high-performance Typhoon interceptor and Tempest derivative, and the Fury/Sea Fury development of the Tempest. All were built in large numbers by Gloster Aircraft. After the war came the Sea Hawk single-seat naval fighter, designed and built by Hawker, but later transferred to Armstrong Whitworth, and the P1067 subsonic jet fighter prototype, which first flew on 20 July 1951. This became the Rolls-Royce Avon-powered Hunter, which was flown in its production form on 16 May 1953 and entered RAF service in July 1954. Hunter production totalled 1,985 aircraft, including licence-production abroad. Subsequent designs carried the Hawker Siddeley name.

Below:
When it entered service with No 43 Sqn in mid-1931, the Hawker Fury became the RAF's first fighter to exceed 200mph in level flight. Powered by a 525hp Rolls-Royce Kestrel engine, 118 Mk 1s and 98 Mk 2s were built for the RAF and export models went to Yugoslavia (16), Persia (22), South Africa (six), Spain (three), Portugal (three) and Norway (one). Illustrated is the first Portuguese Fury. *M. J. Hooks Collection*

Bottom:
The Hawker Sea Fury was the Royal Navy's last piston-engined fighter; powered by a 2,550hp Bristol Centaurus engine, the type entered service in 1947. Total production for the Navy amounted to 615 single-seaters plus 60 two-seat T. Mk 20s. Overseas deliveries were made to The Netherlands (22), Iraq (60), Pakistan (98) and Egypt (12), many of these being land-based versions. Fokker also built Sea Furies under licence, and some surplus RN aircraft went to Burma, Cuba and West Germany.
M. J. Hooks Collection

Below:
Entering Royal Navy service in March 1953, the Hawker Sea Hawk replaced Sea Furies and Attackers, the latter being the Navy's first pure jet aircraft. Powered by the Rolls-Royce Nene turbojet, the Sea Hawk was popular in service and more than 430 were delivered. Additionally, overseas orders covered West Germany (64), The Netherlands (32) and India (24).

Bottom:
The Hawker Hunter is universally acknowledged as a thoroughbred with virtually viceless handling qualities. Well over 1,000 single-seaters were built for the RAF plus some two-seat trainers, and over 400 new aircraft and many ex-RAF refurbished models were sold worldwide. The Hunter was also built in The Netherlands (189) and Belgium (256). XF432 was an Armstrong Whitworth -built F6, which was later converted to FR10. *M. J. Hooks Collection.*

Hawker Siddeley

On 1 July 1963, the Hawker Siddeley Group, then encompassing Hawker, de Havilland, Gloster, Armstrong Whitworth, Armstrong Siddeley, A. V. Roe, Folland, and Blackburn, underwent a major reorganisation into Hawker Siddeley Aviation (HSA) and Hawker Siddeley Dynamics (HSD). Aircraft in development or production took on HS numbers. The HS681 (formerly AW681) jet V/STOL freighter project came to nothing, but the HS121 Trident (formerly DH121), the HS125 business jet (ex-DH125) and the HS650 Argosy freighter (previously AW650), were all built in numbers, as was the HS748 (Avro 748) and the de Havilland DH106

Comet. The Comet was the world's first jet airliner and after production finished in 1964, Hawker Siddeley developed the Comet 4C into the Nimrod anti-submarine warfare and surveillance aircraft, first flown in June 1968. The 748's maiden flight on 24 June 1960 was the beginning of a long production run which finally ended in 1989. Powered by two Rolls-Royce Dart turboprops, the 50-seat HS748 was produced in several series and included Andover CMk1 variant for the Royal Air Force. The 100-seat Trident 1C, powered by three Rolls-Royce Spey turbofans, made its first flight on 9 January 1962 at Hatfield and entered service with British European Airways on 1 April 1964. It was followed in subsequent years by the 115-seat Trident 1E, the improved

Top:
A low-level subsonic attack aircraft designed by the Blackburn company, the Buccaneer subsequently came under the Hawker Siddeley Group. First deliveries of 60 Mk 1s to the Royal Navy began in March 1961 and the South African Air Force received 16 S50s. The first Royal Navy S Mk 2s followed in March 1965; total production reached 133, some being delivered new to the RAF while others were transferred from the Navy when that service ceased to operate standard fixed-wing combat aircraft.

Above:
One of Britain's big successes in postwar civil aircraft has been the de Havilland DH125, subsequently the HS125 and now the BAe 125. First flown in 1962, it became an immediate success with worldwide sales, notably in the fiercely competitive North American executive jet market. Total sales approach 900; illustrated is a 125-800 used by Rega, the Swiss Air Ambulance service.

Top right:
Another very successful postwar product was the Avro 748 turboprop airliner which became the HS748. Powered by two Rolls-Royce Darts, well over 350 were sold worldwide to civil and military customers. As a military freighter with rear loading ramp it became the Andover C Mk 1 with the RAF and RNZAF.

Right:
The Trident originated as a de Havilland project in response to a requirement from BEA, which put the type 1C into service on 1 April 1964. It is best known for making the first ever automatic landing on a scheduled service on 16 May 1967. Kuwait Airways bought three Trident 1Es, distinguished by a higher all-up weight and more powerful Rolls-Royce Spey turbofan engines.

Trident 2E, and the high-capacity, 179-seat Trident 3B. The Trident was designed from the outset for automatic landing in all weathers and made its first fully-automatic landing at Bedford on 5 March 1963. Total production was 69 aircraft.

The 6–8 seat HS125 business jet, fitted with two Bristol Siddeley Viper turbojets, made its maiden flight on 13 August 1962 and was produced in a series of civil versions and as the Dominie TMk1 for the RAF, serving principally as a navigation trainer. Both the Trident and HS125 were built at Hatfield, while the 74 Argosies were manufactured at Baginton, Coventry, and Bitteswell Aerodrome, Warwickshire, in civil 100 and 200 Series, and as the Argosy CMk1 for the RAF. Hawker Siddeley also continued development of the Folland Gnat and the Blackburn-designed Buccaneer, but its most prestigious product was the Harrier, the western world's only operational fixed-wing V/STOL strike fighter. Developed from the P1127 Kestrel, which first flew (tethered) on 21 October 1960, the Harrier family first entered service with the RAF on 1 April 1969. Early versions included GR1, GR1A and GR3 close-support and tactical reconnaissance aircraft, all powered with

Below:
The P1127 Kestrel experimental V/STOL tactical fighter was developed into the highly-successful Harrier, still the western world's only operational fixed-wing vertical/short take-off strike aircraft.

the Rolls-Royce Pegasus vectored-thrust turbofan engine, followed by a two-seat development version, first flown on 24 April 1969, leading to the Harrier T2, T2A and T4. On 29 April 1977, both Hawker Siddeley Aviation and Hawker Siddeley Dynamics vanished in an enforced merger with BAC and Scottish Aviation to form British Aerospace.

Hendy

Established at Shoreham by Basil B. Henderson in 1929, the Hendy Aircraft Co had a short existence, being absorbed into Parnall Aircraft Ltd in 1935. In the intervening years, the company built the Model 281 Hobo, a single-seat cantilever monoplane powered by a 35hp ABC Scorpion II engine, and the Cirrus Hermes I-powered Model 302, a two-seater flown in the 1930 King's Cup race. Basil Henderson also designed the Model 3308, a fast tandem two-seat cabin monoplane first flown in July 1934, which became known as the Parnall Heck.

Heston

The Heston Aircraft Co Ltd was formed in June 1934 when it acquired the assets of Comper Aircraft Ltd. Its first aircraft was the Type 1 Phoenix, a five-seat wooden monoplane designed by George Cornwall. Although generally of conventional construction, the Phoenix was the first British high-wing monoplane to

feature the Dowty hydraulically-operated, inward-retracting undercarriage, giving the aircraft exceptionally graceful lines when in flight. It first flew on 18 August 1935, but only six were built over the next four years. Other types to be completed at Heston included the three-seat Hordern-Richmond Autoplane, T1/37 military trainer, and the Type 5 Racer, built in 1940 for an attempt at the world's air speed record. The Racer had a very short career, however, being damaged beyond repair on its first flight on 12 June 1940. During the war, the company

serviced many subcontracts, and after peace returned flew the A2/45 two-seat observation aircraft in August 1947.

Hillson

Following demonstration flights in the UK in 1935, the woodworking firm of F. Hills & Sons Ltd acquired a licence to built the Czech E114 Praga, an all-wooden light aircraft, at its works at Trafford Park in Manchester. Production of the Hillson Praga began

in 1936 and ended in 1939 after the completion of 28 airframes. Hills built two other, this time indigenous two-seat aircraft, the Pennine and Helvellyn, both designed by Norman Sykes. The former was a high-wing cabin monoplane built in 1937 with a 36hp Praga B engine, and the latter a mid-wing training aircraft, powered by a 90hp Blackburn Cirrus Minor 1 engine and completed in 1939. Two years later, Hillson produced the ambitious Bi-Mono, a slip-wing research aircraft, capable of taking off as a biplane, and flying missions as a monoplane.

Hunting

When Percival Aircraft Ltd was renamed Hunting Percival Aircraft Ltd in 1954, it continued production of the P50 Prince, P56 Provost, P66 Sea Prince, Pembroke and President models, as well as the P84 Jet Provost, which became the standard two-seat basic jet trainer for the RAF. More than 450 were built and remained in service until being replaced by the Hawk on a gradual basis from 1976. In 1957, another retitling occurred when the Percival name was dropped

Top:
With major design features from the piston Provost, the Hunting Jet Provost was a natural successor and became the first aircraft in which pupils could receive all instruction on a jet type, from first flight to solo and after. Following a small batch of T1s, the main production model, the T3, entered service in June 1959, and over 300 were built for the RAF and export markets.

Above:
The No 4 Biplane, powered by a 50hp Gnome engine, was operated by its own flying school at Hendon. It had an endurance of three hours.
Philip Jarrett Collection

altogether, but Hunting Aircraft Ltd itself then came under the control of the newly-formed British Aircraft Corporation in September 1960. While it continued project work, comprising the H126 Jet-flap research aircraft and the H107, a 44/55-seat jetliner study which led to the BAC One-Eleven, it closed its design office in 1965.

London & Provincial

The London & Provincial Aviation Co was established at Hendon in October 1913 and initially built the Caudron GIII trainer under licence. In 1916, A. A. Fletcher, who had joined from Martinsyde in 1916, designed the No 4 biplane trainer, powered by a single 50hp Gnome engine; followed by the School Biplane, fitted with the 80hp, later 100hp Anzani. A total of 12 were produced in 1916/17.

Luton

In 1936, Luton Aircraft Ltd of Barton-in-the-Clay, Bedfordshire, flew the Buzzard I, a single-seat open-cockpit wooden ultralight, powered by one 35hp Anzani and designed by C. H. Latimer-Needham. This was rebuilt the following year with short-span wings and enclosed cockpit as the Buzzard II. The tandem-wing LA2 never flew, but its fuselage and other components were incorporated into the LA3, which was itself redesigned for home-assembly as the LA4 Minor. The first was built at the company's Phoenix Works at Gerrards Cross, Buckinghamshire, and fitted with a 40hp ABC Scorpion, but subsequent models were home-built from drawings and fitted with many different engines. A hangar fire at the Phoenix Works in 1943 destroyed the single example of the LA5 Major, a two-seat cabin type first flown on 4 March 1939, and also spelt the end for the company. C. H. Latimer-Needham founded a new

Above:
A single-seat ultra-light, the first Luton Minor was built in 1936 with a 35hp Anzani engine. Other examples followed with a variety of engines and a number have been home-built postwar, of which G-ATFW is a typical example. *M. J. Hooks Collection*

company at Cranleigh, Surrey, in March 1958, appropriately named Phoenix Aircraft Ltd, which acquired the rights for the Minor and Major. Both designs were improved, the first as the LA4A Minor, and built in the UK and in several countries across the world.

Marendaz

D. M. K. Marendaz designed a small number of high-speed low-wing monoplanes in the mid-1930s, beginning with the four-seat MKII in 1935. This gave way to the MkIII, another four-seater, but with a retractable undercarriage and a more powerful 200hp de Havilland Gipsy VI engine. Both were built by International Aircraft & Engineering Ltd at its Cordwallis Works in Maidenhead, Berkshire, but when these were destroyed by fire in June 1937, the designer formed his own Marendaz Aircraft Ltd at Barton-in-the-Clay, Bedfordshire. Only one more type was produced before the company ceased operations. This was the two-seat Blackburn Cirrus Minor I-powered Marendaz Trainer, first flown on 11 December 1939. Only one aircraft was built.

Martin-Baker

Capt James Martin's early attempt at aircraft design and construction with the M1 side-by-side two-seater built at Denham in 1929, was short-lived, the depression forcing him to give up his venture. In 1934, however, he joined with Capt Valentine Baker to set up Martin-Baker Aircraft Ltd and produced the MB1, an all-metal experimental two-seater, to demonstrate his own system of lattice girder construction. Only one was built and was followed by the MB2 fighter, first flown with a 1,000hp Napier Dagger engine on 3 August 1938, and built at Heston, where the company had moved its operation in 1937. On 31 August 1942, the Sabre-powered MB3 made its début and the last product was the MB5, considered one of the best piston-engined fighters built. The company then ceased aircraft construction and devoted its resources to the development of ejection seats, which continues to this day.

Martinsyde

Based at Brooklands, Weybridge, Surrey, H. P. Martin and George Handasyde began, in 1908, building a number of undistinguished monoplanes. However, they came into prominence at the beginning of World War 1, then reformed as Martinsyde Ltd, when producing a fast biplane, the S1 Scout, first flown on 27 June 1912 and powered by an 80hp Gnome rotary engine. Although 60 were built, the Scout achieved limited success and was soon superseded on the production line by the G100 Elephant which, although conceived as a scout, went into military service in 1916 as a long-range, high-speed

Above:
The four-seat Marendaz III was quite an advanced concept for 1937, but unfortunately never went into production. The first, uncompleted, prototype was destroyed in a factory fire while the second, G-AFGG, although exhibited at the 1938 RAeS garden party, was never completed. The engine was a DH Gipsy VI of 200hp. *M. J. Hooks Collection*

Top right and centre right:
Well known as builders of ejection seats, Martin-Baker built several aircraft between 1934 and 1936, but none were selected for production. Illustrated are the MB3 with a 2,000hp Napier Sabre engine and the company's last aircraft, the brilliant MB5 of 1946 with a 2,340hp Rolls-Royce Griffon engine driving contra-rotating propellers and with a top speed of 460mph. The advent of the jet effectively ruined its chances.

Bottom right:
A number of ex-service Martinsyde biplanes were civil registered in 1919/20. Among them was this conversion of a F4, one of two powered by a 300hp ADC Nimbus engine and known as Nimbus Martinsydes. Both flew in the 1926 King's Cup race, while -EBOJ, further modified, won the High Powered Handicap at 141mph the following year. *M. J. Hooks Collection*

bomber. Next came the F1, F2 and F3 prototypes, followed by the F4 Buzzard. This single-seat fighter came too late for operations in the war, and some of the 280 aircraft produced were sold to the RAF and foreign air forces after 1918, while others were converted to civil use with several engines and varying configurations, simply known as the

Right:
The first production Miles Hawk, G-ACHJ, was the forerunner of a whole series of Hawks of different models. Normally a two-seater, it was flown in several races as a single-seater. The engine was a 95hp ADC Cirrus 3A. *M. J. Hooks Collection*

Below:
Developed from the Miles Hawk Major, the Hawk Trainer in military service became the Magister. Almost 1,300 were built for flying clubs, the RAF and overseas customers. Postwar, a considerable number were converted from surplus RAF stocks for civilian use and 100 were built under licence in Turkey. L83338, illustrated with its blind flying hood folded, was subsequently sold to Argentina. *M. J. Hooks Collection*

Bottom:
Miles built 50 Whitney Straights with a unit price of £985. Powered by a 130hp DH Gipsy Major engine, it was a popular two-seater, first flown in May 1936. A number were impressed during World War 2 and nine survived, of which two exist in Britain.
M. J. Hooks Collection

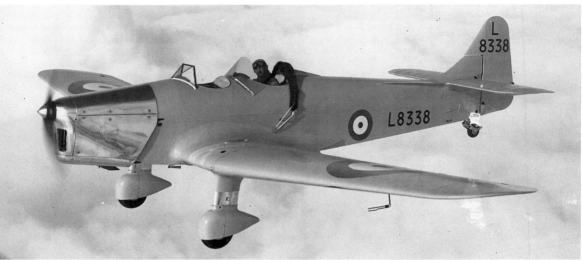

Martinsydes. It was not long before the company felt the full effect of the postwar slump, forcing it into liquidation in 1921. The remaining airframes went to the Aircraft Disposal Co Ltd, which embarked on a redesign, resulting in the ADC1 and the Nimbus. The last civil Martinsyde, the AV1, was assembled at Croydon in 1931 by A. D. C. Aircraft Ltd, Aircraft Disposal's successor.

Miles

Miles Aircraft Ltd was established in October 1943 to take over the business of Phillips & Powis Aircraft Ltd, itself founded in January 1931 as Phillips & Powis (Reading) Ltd. The Woodley Aerodrome, Reading-based company built several aircraft

designed by F. G. Miles. Of note were the M2 Hawk two-seat light touring aircraft first flown on 29 March 1933, followed by the M2F Hawk Major, M3 Falcon and the five-seat M4 Merlin. All were powered by de Havilland Gipsy engines and won many racing honours, as did the single-seat M5 Sparrowhawk. Miles' first aircraft, the M1 Satyr wooden aerobatic

Below:
The Miles Messenger four-seat liaison aircraft had STOL characteristics and two models were built with either a 155hp Blackburn Cirrus Major 3 or a 145hp DH Gipsy Major engine. A number saw military service, one being used by Field Marshal Montgomery, and production continued postwar for the civil market until 1948 when the 81st was delivered.

Left:
The first Miles Aerovan light freighter flew in January 1945 and entered production in 1946. Fifty-four were laid down, but the last two were not completed. Standard engine was the 155hp Blackburn Cirrus Major, but two were fitted with 195hp Lycomings. At least 27 were destroyed in crashes and a further five blown over in gales, but nevertheless the type was considered successful by its operators. UO248/G-AGOZ was the prototype.

Above:
Three NAC Firecrackers with a 715ehp Pratt & Whitney Canada PT6A-25 turboprop engine were built, following a piston-engined version, and were evaluated with the competing Pilatus PC-9 and Shorts Tucano for an RAF order subsequently won by Shorts. Two Firecrackers were subsequently acquired by Specialist Flying Training at Carlisle, but neither are now in use. *M. J. Hooks Collection*

Right:
First flown in December 1981 and designed by Desmond Norman with financial support from the National Research Development Corporation, the Fieldmaster was intended for agricultural, oil pollution clearance and firefighting work — the prototype is shown picking up water with a scoop which could refill the tank in less than a minute. In this form it becomes the Firemaster and several were used in France to fight forest fires. *M. J. Hooks Collection*

biplane, was built by George Parnall at Yate in Gloucestershire. In 1939, the Woodley factory was enlarged to handle a sizeable contract for the M9A Master, a high-speed advanced trainer monoplane, powered by a 720hp Rolls-Royce Kestrel 30 engine. Other types built in large numbers in the late 1930s and early war years included the M11 Whitney Straight side-by-side two-seat cabin monoplane; the M14 Magister, a two-seat primary trainer based on the Hawk; the more powerful M19 Master II and M27 Master III developments; and the M33 Monitor target-towing aircraft. The prototype M28 Mercury, a high-speed four-seater, was developed into the M38 Messenger, which first flew on 12 September 1942 and was sold to the RAF and private owners.

In 1944, F. G. Miles designed the M57 Aerovan short-haul utility transport to carry bulky loads. First flown on 26 January 1945, the Aerovan was a high-wing monoplane with a capacious fuselage, featuring a hinged rear door and triple fins supported by a boom, and could carry up to nine passengers or one tonne of freight. Fifty-two Aerovans were built, but its larger developments, the M68 Boxcar and M71 Merchantman did not make it into production. The last to be built at Woodley in numbers was the M65 Gemini, a four-seat cabin monoplane derived from the M38 Messenger. An interesting project, the M52 supersonic research aircraft, was cancelled in January 1946. In November the following year, Miles Aircraft Ltd went into receivership. F. G. Miles set up a new company, F. G. Miles Ltd, at Redhill in June 1951, but soon moved operations to Shoreham on the South Coast where he continued development of the HDM105 Aerovan, so designated because it had a new high aspect ratio metal wing designed by Hurel-Dubois of Villacoublay, France. It first flew on 30 March 1957, but never made it in to service. The final projects, before being absorbed into Beagle-Miles in October 1960, were the HDM106 Caravan utility freighter and the M100 Student, a two-seat trainer powered by a single 880lb st Blackburn Turbomeca Marbor turbojet.

NDN

After leaving Britten-Norman, N. D. (Desmond) Norman founded the NDN Aircraft Ltd at Sandown, Isle of Wight, in 1976 to develop the NDN 1 Firecracker turboprop trainer. Powered by a 260hp Avco Lycoming piston engine, the Firecracker first flew on 26 May 1977, but failed to win any production orders. This was followed by the tandem seat NDN 6 Fieldmaster, a large agricultural aircraft which made its first flight on 17 December 1981, powered by a single 750hp Pratt & Whitney PT6A-34AG turboprop engine. A turbine version of the Firecracker, the NDN 1T, flew on 1 September 1983 and, for a short time, became the Hunting Firecracker. On 22 July 1985, NDN was renamed Norman Aeroplane Co (NAC), simultaneously transferring its production centre to Barry in South Wales. To the Fieldmaster had been added the NAC 1 Freelance multi-purpose utility aircraft with folding wings (first flown 29 September 1984), but NAC called in the receiver in July 1988. Production of the Fieldmaster was transferred to Brooklands Aircraft Ltd for a short time, before Irish-based Croplease Ltd acquired the rights in April 1989. Since 1992, the aircraft is being produced by EPA Aircraft Co, which offers it as the EPA NAC 6 Fieldmaster for agricultural work, and as the Firemaster for firefighting.

Parnall

The Bristol woodworking firm of George Parnall & Sons obtained contracts for wartime construction of the Avro 504, Shorts 827 and Fairey Hamble Baby, building a total of 200 aircraft. The first to carry the Parnall name were the Scout and Puffin prototypes, and after Harold Bolas joined as chief designer in 1917, Parnall produced the Panther, a two-seat spotter and reconnaissance biplane, 150 of which were built by the British and Colonial Aeroplane Co at Filton between 1919 and 1922. Aircraft design and construction ceased following the sale of the company to W. & T. Avery, but most of the original design team joined up in 1920 to form George Parnall & Co Ltd, which then proceeded to create 18 different designs. Among these were the Plover, a single-seat carrier-borne biplane fighter built at its Coliseum Works in Bristol, and a number of ultra-light biplanes and monoplanes for the 1920s Lympne Trials, all designed by Harold Bolas. These included the single-seat wooden Pixie I and II monos and the two-seat Pixie IIIA biplane, later converted to monoplanes as the Pixie III. The two-seat Imp and Elf biplanes first flew in 1928 and 1929, by which time production had shifted to Yate Aerodrome in Gloucestershire. After the establishment of Parnall Aircraft Ltd from the amalgamation of George Parnall & Co, Hendy Aircraft Co and the engineering firm of Nash Thompson Ltd, the company developed the Heck, which had originated and first flown in July 1934 as the two-seat Hendy 3308, into the Heck 2C. This differed primarily in having three seats and a fixed spatted undercarriage, replacing the manually-operated retractable system. Only seven were produced and flown in the King's Cup races and on RAF communications duties. A two-seat dual-control trainer version, known as the Parnall 328 or Heck 3, appeared in 1939, but did not go into production.

Above:
Parnall, which took over Hendy Aircraft in 1935, built the Hendy Heck, a two-seat tourer with a 200hp DH Gipsy VI engine. The prototype, G-ACTC, was in fact built by Westland, but Parnall followed it with seven production aircraft. The last survivor, G-AEGI, was scrapped after being cut in half in a ground collision at Wolverhampton in 1950 when Spitfire G-AISU (now with the Battle of Britain Memorial Flight as AB910) taxied into it. *M. J. Hooks Collection*

Percival

Australian Capt Edgar W. Percival's attempt at aircraft design resulted in the three-seat, wooden low-wing Gull of 1932, which achieved a remarkable career as a racer and led to the establishment of the Percival Aircraft Co Ltd by Percival himself, in association with Lt-Cdr E. W. B. Leake. Early production aircraft were built by George Parnall & Co at Yate Aerodrome, but in June 1934 the company established its own works at Gravesend, Kent. The early Cirrus Hermes IV-powered Gulls were superseded by the Gull Major and Gull Six models, which had Gipsy Major and Gipsy VI engines respectively. A specially-built single-seat racer, the Mew Gull, came next, followed by the four-seat Vega Gull in November 1935. A year later, the company was restructured as Percival Aircraft Ltd, concurrently with a move to larger premises at Luton Airport, Bedfordshire, and the design of its first twin-engined aircraft, the Q6, with Gipsy VI engines, retractable undercarriage and seating for up to six passengers. Twenty-seven aircraft were built, including some for the RAF which, together with the Royal Navy, also took delivery of more than 1,000 three-seat Proctor navigational and radio trainers and communications aircraft based on the Vega Gull. Some were built by

F. Hills & Sons Ltd at Manchester, and many were later converted for civil use.

In the immediate postwar years, Percival produced the P40 Prentice three-seat basic trainer and the five-seat all-metal P48 Merganser prototype, which led to the P50 Prince medium feeder transport, first flown on 13 May 1948, powered by two 520hp Alvis Leonides engines. Accommodation was provided for up to 12 passengers. Further developments of the basic airframe produced the P54 Survey Prince, military P66 Pembroke and the six-seat executive President. In 1944, Percival Aircraft Ltd had come under the control of the Hunting Group. When it was renamed Hunting Percival Aircraft Ltd in 1954, Edgar W. Percival left and started a new company at Stapleford Tawney, Essex, building 21 EP9 utility aircraft before selling out to Samlesbury Engineering, itself reformed as the Lancashire Aircraft Co in 1960. Production of the EP9 as the Lancashire Prospector continued until 1963.

Top:
The prototype and first production batch of 24 Percival Gulls were built by Parnall, but in 1934 Percival established a factory at Gravesend where 22 were built before the company moved to Luton in 1936. Various engines from 130 to 205hp were installed in the Gull/Vega Gull family of which 89 were built. G-ACPA was the last Parnall-built Gull.

Above:
The Percival Proctor began life as a strengthened Vega Gull, built to an Air Ministry specification. A total of 1,287 were built in six variants and were used by the RAF as communications and radio training aircraft. A purely civil version, the Mk V four-seater, was produced postwar and enjoyed considerable success. Illustrated is the one-off Proctor VI floatplane built for the Hudson's Bay Co. *M. J. Hooks Collection*

G-AHTB

G-AOK

Top:
Percival's Q6 was essentially a twin-engined enlarged version of the Vega Gull. Flown in September 1937, it had 205hp DH Gipsy VI engines and accommodation for a crew of two and four passengers. Initial price was quoted as £4,550; total production was 27, including seven for the RAF and several export models. The sole survivor is being slowly restored to flying condition in the Isle of Man. *M. J. Hooks Collection*

Above:
A total of 483 Percival Prentice trainers were built; of these, 360 went to the RAF, 100 to Argentina, three to Lebanon and 20 to India where a further 42 were built. Powered by a 250hp DH Gipsy Queen engine, Prentices entered RAF service in 1947 and when they became surplus from 1953 Aviation Traders bought 252 for the civilian market but only 25 were converted, one of which is shown. *M. J. Hooks Collection*

Top right:
The Hunting Percival Sea Prince was a military version of the Prince feeder liner and was ordered for the Royal Navy as a communications aircraft (C Mk 1) and flying classroom (T Mk 1). Total production was 48. Illustrated are the first and last T Mk 1s, then based at Culdrose.

Right:
Edgar Percival formed a new company in 1955 to build the EP9 agricultural aircraft and a batch of 20 was begun, the first flying in December 1955. Powerplant was a 270hp Lycoming GO-480. In 1958 a new company, Lancashire Aircraft Corporation, was set up and the type named Prospector. In all, 28 were built including one uncompleted airframe; a number were exported, mostly to Australia. G-ARDG was a one-off Mk II with a 375hp Armstrong Siddeley Cheetah engine. *M. J. Hooks Collection*

Winner of the contract for a new RAF basic trainer, the Hunting Percival Provost was powered by a 550hp Alvis Leonides engine. It served from October 1953 until October 1969, when the last airworthy Provost, WW397, flew to Halton. Some 387 had been built and a number went to overseas air forces. Illustrated is an armed Provost of the Union of Burma Air Force. *M. J. Hooks Collection*

Right:
The Boultbee-designed three-seat Pobjoy Pirate had a poor performance and was scrapped in 1936, having spent only just over one hour in the air since first flown in June 1935. *Philip Jarrett Collection*

Pobjoy

Engaged solely in the production of aero engines from 1930, Pobjoy Airmotors Ltd of Rochester, Kent, engaged Harold Boultbee, whose Civilian Aircraft Co Ltd had ceased operations, to design an aircraft using its own 90hp Niagara III engine. Known as the Pirate, this three-seat plywood-covered monoplane with folding wings first flew on 25 June 1935, but no further examples were built. In that same month, the company was reorganised as Pobjoy Airmotors & Aircraft Ltd, to reflect more accurately its extended activities, acquiring an exclusive licence to build the Short Scion commercial monoplane. Pobjoy built a total of seven aircraft, but did not take up its licence to follow on with the Scion Senior.

Portsmouth

Originally founded in June 1932 as Portsmouth, Southsea & Isle of Wight Aviation to operate air services to the Isle of Wight, the company undertook repair and overhaul of RAF aircraft during the war. In 1943, it was restructured as Portsmouth Aviation Ltd and began aircraft design and construction at Portsmouth City Airport, which it managed. The

Above:
The Portsmouth Aerocar Major flew in June 1947 with 155hp Blackburn Cirrus Major engines. It seated five passengers and was quite an advanced design, but the concept did not attract any orders and it was scrapped in 1950. *M. J. Hooks Collection*

prototype Aerocar Major, a twin-boom, high-wing monoplane seating up to five passengers in a pod type fuselage and powered by twin 155hp Blackburn Cirrus Major III engines, made its aerial début on 18 June 1947. Although plans were made to produce four different versions, the Aerocar Major elicited little interest and never went into production.

Robinson

In October 1929, Capt P. G. Robinson formed the Robinson Aircraft Co Ltd and set about building a side-by-side two-seater light aircraft at his workshop in Croydon. Designed by John Kenworthy and powered by the 75hp ABC Hornet flat-four engine, the Redwing I made its début in May 1930 and was followed in October by the slightly more powerful

Redwing II, with an 80hp Genet II radial engine. In April 1931, the company was reorganised as Redwing Aircraft Ltd and on 10 March 1932 the Croydon works were closed and production transferred to Blue Barns Aerodrome, Colchester, Essex. Only two more Redwings were built, including the sole Redwing III, which featured a reduced wingspan and better aerodynamics. Redwing later moved to Redhill to concentrate on subcontract work.

Royal Aircraft Factory

Although having no authority to build aircraft, Her Majesty's Balloon Factory at Farnborough, Hampshire, nevertheless embarked on the design of six types: BE (Bleriot Experimental tractor type),

BS (Bleriot Scout fast single-seat tractor), FE (Farman Experimental pusher), RE (Reconnaissance Experimental two-seat tractor), SE (Santos Experimental tail-first or canard), and TE (Tatin Experimental propeller behind tail). Its first design was the FE1, developed by Geoffrey de Havilland, who had joined as chief test pilot in December 1910. On 1 April 1911, the establishment was renamed Army Aircraft Factory, the Royal prefix being added on 1 April 1912. The most notable early designs, the BE1 two-seat tractor biplane and FE2 two-seat pusher (first flown on 1 January 1912 and 18 August 1911 respectively), produced a total of around 5,500 BE2a/b/c/d/e reconnaissance and FE2a/b/d pusher fighters, built at Farnborough and by more than 20 other companies. Other types built in numbers include the RE5, RE7, RE8 and the SE5/5a fighter, the last-named designed by Harry Folland, John Kenworthy and Frank Goodden, achieving a production run of 5,205 aircraft. Folland also designed the world's then fastest aircraft, the SE4, in 1914, which reached a speed of 135mph. The factory altogether produced 533 aircraft of 28 different types, but after the formation of the Royal Air Force in April 1918, it was renamed Royal Aircraft Establishment, devoted solely to research and testing.

Saunders-Roe

In 1928 Sir Alliot Verdon Roe, having left A. V. Roe & Co, joined with John Lord in acquiring a controlling interest in S. E. Saunders Ltd, which had built a small number of amphibious aircraft, such as the Kittiwake and Medina, at East Cowes, Isle of Wight, since the end of World War 1. The first aircraft of the new company, now named Saunders-Roe Ltd, was the Saro A17 Cutty Sark, a twin-engined, four-seat flying

Above:
One of the great fighters of World War 1 was the RAF SE5A and more than 5,200 of this variant were built, engines being the 200hp Hispano-Suiza, Wolseley Viper or Wolseley Adder. Several SE5As were civil registered after the war and some were used for skywriting. Three of these survive, two in museums and one in flying condition, restored by the RAF.

boat introduced on 4 July 1929. The A19 Cloud was built between 1930 and 1933 in two basic forms, as a civil eight-seater and as a military trainer for the RAF, production totalling 21 aircraft, but the contemporary three-engined A21 Windhover amphibian proved less successful. Other prewar flying boats included the London reconnaissance biplane, which entered RAF Coastal Command service in 1937, and the Lerwick monoplane, which joined the London with Coastal Command in 1939. Saunders-Roe's flying boat era reached its zenith on 20 August 1952 with the first flight of the giant SR45 Princess. This was an all-metal flying boat designed by H. Knowler, capable of carrying 220 passengers a distance of more than 5,000 miles. Power was provided by ten 3,780hp Bristol Proteus 600 turboprop engines, arranged in four coupled pairs and two single units. Three were ordered for BOAC, but never entered service. Saunders-Roe projected the Duchess, a 92-passenger jet-powered flying boat in 1950, but had already diversified into small helicopters after taking over the Eastleigh-based Cierva Autogiro Company in 1951, starting with the Skeeter, a two-seat development of the Cierva W14. In 1958, the company began building an all-metal five-seat helicopter, designated P531, but was then taken over by Westland Aircraft in 1959.

Above:
Saunders-Roe built 12 Cutty Sark amphibians between 1929 and 1935, eight of which were UK-registered. Single examples went to the Royal New Zealand Air Force, Hong Kong, Australia and the Marine Aircraft Experimental Establishment, Felixstowe. Three of the UK-registered examples were sold, to Japan, Singapore and San Domingo. A variety of engines from 105 to 140hp were used. *M. J. Hooks Collection*

Below:
Larger than the Cutty Sark, the Saunders-Roe Cloud followed the earlier model and was launched in 1930. Twenty-one were built, again with various engines and, of these, 17 went to the RAF and four to British civil marks. The last production Cloud went to the Czech airline CSA and was powered with Walter Pollux Engines. Shown on take-off, its fuselage survives in a Czech museum. *M. J. Hooks Collection*

Left:
At the time of its construction, the Saunders-Roe Princess was the heaviest all-metal passenger transport and the biggest all-metal flying boat built. Technically successful, it was powered by 10 Bristol Proteus gas turbines in four-coupled pairs and two singles. Flown in August 1952, only the prototype was completed, two others being partly finished and the programme ended by June 1954. The two semi-complete Princesses were broken up in 1965 and G-ALUN followed in April 1967. *M. J. Hooks Collection*

Above:
The Saunders-Roe Skeeter light helicopter flew in
October 1948 and was intended for civil and military
use. A number of prototypes were built and after
considerable military trials the Skeeter went into
production for the Army Air Corps. Sixty-four were built
for the AAC, plus 10 for the German Army and Navy.
Production aircraft had 215hp DH Gipsy Major
engines.

Below:
Scottish Aviation followed its successful STOL single-
engine Pioneer with the Twin Pioneer powered by 550
or 640hp Alvis Leonides engines. Deliveries of 39 to
the RAF were made between 1958 and 1961 and a
further 22 were built for civil operators.
M. J. Hooks Collection

Scottish Aviation

In June 1935, the Marquess of Clydesdale and David McIntyre, both intrepid flyers, played a leading role in the establishment of Scottish Aviation Ltd at the new Prestwick Aerodrome, initially to operate a flying school. After opening its first factory in 1938, the company ventured into aircraft overhaul, modifications and subcontract work, before producing two designs of its own after the war. These were the Pioneer (also known as the Prestwick Pioneer) and the Twin Pioneer, both of which served with the RAF and civil operators. The Pioneer started life as a three-seat communications aircraft, but was redeveloped into the larger Pioneer 2 in 1950, when the original military requirement failed to materialise. The triple-finned 16-seat Twin Pioneer first flew on 25 June 1955 and went on to provide sterling service in a variety of roles both at home and abroad. Production totalled 59 Pioneers and 87 Twin Pioneers. Subsequently, Scottish Aviation took over development and production of the Jetstream light transport, following the closure of Handley Page in 1970, and the Bulldog trainer when a similar fate befell Beagle Aircraft in December 1969. On 29 April 1977, Scottish Aviation was nationalised and became part of British Aerospace.

Shorts

Ballooning, which had been an enthusiastic pursuit of the three Short brothers — Albert Eustace, Horace Leonard and Hugh Oswald — since 1897, was no longer enough once the Wright brothers had proven that powered flight was possible. Short Brothers

Above:
Beagle's Bulldog, a military trainer development of the Pup, was taken over by Scottish Aviation after Beagle collapsed in 1970. Powered by a 200hp Avco-Lycoming 10-360 engine, illustrated is a Malaysian Air Force Bulldog. *M. J. Hooks Collection*

(Rochester & Bedford) Ltd was formally established in November 1908, since when the company has been at the forefront of British aviation. Biplanes came first, but its connections with seaplanes started as early as 1911. Success with the torpedo bombers of World War 1, all built at Shorts' Seaplane Works in Rochester, led to a long line of often remarkable all-metal flying boats, pioneered with the landplane Silverstreak, which first flew on 20 August 1920. Of historic importance was the S8 Calcutta, the first flying boat with a stressed-skin metal hull. Designed by Arthur Gouge and based on the experience gained with the Singapore I of 1926, the three-engined, 15-seat Calcutta was operated on Imperial Airways' Mediterranean sector of the Empire route from 16 April 1929. From the Calcutta, Shorts produced the Rangoon as a long-range reconnaissance type for the RAF. The S17 Kent, an enlarged four-engined development of the Calcutta flew on 24 February 1931, followed on 30 June 1932 by the S14 Sarafand patrol flying boat, then the second largest in the world after the Dornier DoX. Odd ones out during the 1930s were the S16 Scion, a twin-engined landplane for five passengers; the larger Scion Senior; and the Scylla, a landplane derivative of the Kent.

Shorts made a great breakthrough in 1934 when Imperial Airways placed an order for 14 flying boats,

Top:
Five Short Calcuttas were built for Imperial Airways' Mediterranean section of the route to India. Powered by three 540hp Bristol Jupiter engines, the Calcuttas entered service initially on UK routes in 1928. Accommodation was for 15 passengers and there was a buffet service. The last survivor was scrapped in 1939. *M. J. Hooks Collection*

Above:
Designed as a feeder liner, the Short Scion flew in September 1933 with two 75hp Pobjoy engines; production aircraft had 85 or 90hp Pobjoy Niagaras. Five passengers could be carried and of the 15 Scions built, four went to Australia. The type's popularity led to the enlarged 10-seat Scion Senior with four Pobjoys, of which six were built, three going to India as float-planes. *M. J. Hooks Collection*

later increased to 28, straight from the drawing board. Designated the S23 C-Class Empire flying boat, this most famous of all prewar flying boats first flew on 4 July 1936 and helped to expand the Empire air mail routes, being able to carry 24 passengers in luxury, as well as 1.5 tonnes of mail. On long-haul flights, sleeping accommodation was provided for 16 passengers. New Bristol Perseus XIIC engines, increased take-off weight and greater range was provided with the S30, and a further development was the S26 G-Class flying boat, first launched in June 1939. The build up of military activities prior to World War 2, when Shorts became involved in manufacturing aircraft of other companies as well as its own, forced the closure of the Rochester works, partly because it became too small, but more pertinently because it was considered too vulnerable to possible German attack. In 1936, therefore, Shorts established a new factory at Queen's Island, Belfast, Northern Ireland. Shorts' own contribution to the war effort included the four-engined S25 Sunderland maritime-patrol and reconnaissance flying boat, later remodelled into the civil Sandringham, and the four-engined Stirling, the first of the RAF's heavy bombers to go into wartime service.

On 23 March 1943, the company was controversially appropriated by the Government and renamed Short Brothers & Harland Ltd, being joined with the Harland & Wolff shipyard. The Sunderland was further developed into the Seaford and its civil version, the S45 Solent, and other postwar types included the Sturgeon high-performance carrier-borne target tug and the SA6 Sealand, an all-metal amphibian carrying up to seven passengers. During the 1950s, Shorts built a number of research aircraft, and in the early 1960s produced the SC7 Skyvan, a box-like light utility aircraft, and the SC5 Belfast, a long-range outsize freighter for the RAF. Shorts later gained a measure of success, especially in the American market, with its 30-seat SD-330 and 36-seat 360 twin-turboprop regional aircraft, first flown on 22 August 1974 and 1 June 1981 respectively. A military version of the 330 was sold to the US Army as the C-23A Sherpa. Shorts also produced the Tucano trainer for the RAF, but this was the last complete aircraft project to be undertaken at Belfast. Since being acquired from the Government by Canada's Bombardier Ltd on 4 October 1989, Shorts has been thriving as a specialist subcontracting division, building aircraft parts and sections for others.

Above:
The Shorts C and G Class Empire flying boats were advanced for their time, and Imperial Airways ordered 28 C class straight from the drawing board. They provided luxury travel on the Empire routes and a total of 45 of different variants were built, of which eight were operated by Qantas (some supplied new, others ex-Imperial) and two by Tasman Empire Airways, New Zealand. Thirteen survived the war but were eventually broken up.

Above:
Shorts' experience with the Empire boats led to the military Sunderland, the most famous maritime aircraft of World War 2. The prototype flew in October 1937 and was the first British flying boat to feature power-operated gun turrets; 749 were built and served with the RAF, the RNZAF and France's Aeronavale. The last of 16 reconditioned for the RNZAF is shown.
M. J. Hooks Collection

Below:
A number of converted Shorts Sunderlands served with BOAC in World War 2 and reopened Empire routes in 1946, but to provide more luxurious accommodation Shorts extensively modified the airframe internally and externally, giving two decks and accommodation for 24 passengers. The type was named Sandringham and of the 27 conversions 11 went to BOAC, seven to Argentina, five to DNL, Norway and four to TEAL (New Zealand). The first of the New Zealand aircraft is shown. *M. J. Hooks Collection*

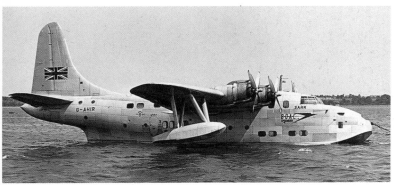

Left:
The ultimate Shorts flying boat to enter service was the Solent, a civilianised version of the military Seaford, and 18 were operated by BOAC between 1948 and 1950, when all flying boat operations ceased. A further four were bought by TEAL. Four Solent variants were built, powered by Bristol Hercules engines from 1,690 to 2,040hp.

Above:
Following production of some Bristol Britannias, Shorts was awarded a contract to build 10 Belfast strategic freighters with four Rolls-Royce Tyne turboprops and similar wings and tails to the Britannia. Belfasts entered service in January 1966 and served well for over 10 years before defence cuts forced the disbandment of No 53 Sqn, the only unit to fly the type. Several Belfasts are in civilian service with cargo carrier HeavyLift.

Below:
More than 150 units of the SC7 Skyvan were sold between 1963, when it made its first flight, and 1986. A low-cost utility aircraft, the Skyvan's fuselage featured unusual bonded light alloy construction for strength and extremely light weight. The rear bottom panel was hinged to form a rear loading ramp.

Right:
Ultimate development of the light freighter concept embodied in the Shorts Skyvan was the Shorts 360, via the 330/Sherpa family. The 360 can carry 36 passengers on short-haul routes and was an immediate success, entering service with US operator Suburban Airlines in December 1982. Like the 330, the 360 made considerable inroads into the US commuter market and 164 were built. Several have recently been sold to the USA for conversions to Sherpas for the USAF.

Winner of a hard-fought contest for a trainer to replace the RAF's Jet Provost was the Embraer Tucano, sponsored by Shorts and being modified by them to meet RAF requirements. First delivery of 130 built for the Service took place in September 1988 to the Central Flying School, and Shorts also built 12 for Kenya and 16 for Kuwait.

Slingsby

Slingsby Aviation Ltd, based at Kirkbymoorside, North Yorkshire, was for a long time associated with sailplanes, but these were discontinued in favour of developing the T67 Firefly two-seat aerobatic trainer. The original T67A version, flown for the first time on 15 May 1981, was a licence-produced Fournier RF6B light aircraft, but this was superseded by the T67B and its military T67M Firefly 160 derivative, built entirely of GFRP and powered by a 116hp Textron Lycoming O-235-N2A flat-four engine. A more powerful 160hp Textron Lycoming engine produced the T67C, while the T67M200, flown on 16 May 1985, has a 200hp AEIO-360-A1E Lycoming. A still more powerful T67M260 version is being delivered to the USAF. Production to date amounts to 140 aircraft.

Above:
Slingsby Aviation continues to manufacture the T67 Firefly series of trainers and at mid-February 1995 had delivered 140, of which 64 were part of a USAF order for 113. Other deliveries have included the RAF (17), Turkey (16), Canada (12), The Netherlands (10), Norway (six), Hong Kong (four), Japan (two) and nine to other customers. *M. J. Hooks Collection*

Below:
Sopwith's two-seat 1½ Strutter, as it became known, entered service with the RNAS in April 1916 and the RFC the following month. Some 1,500 were built in Britain and a further 4,500 in France. A number of other countries used the type including the USA, Russia, Belgium, Romania and Japan. Shown is a take-off using skids from experimental guides on HMS *Vindex*. *M. J. Hooks Collection*

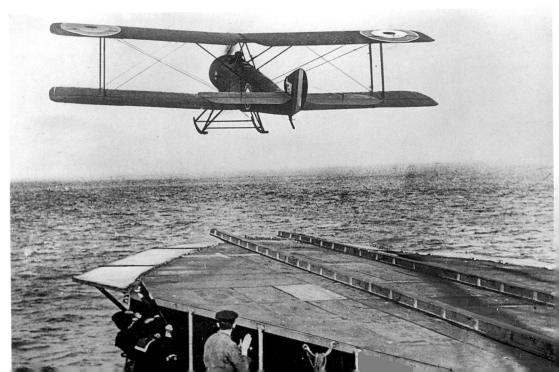

Sopwith

T. O. M. Sopwith, a well-known pioneer pilot, founded The Sopwith Aviation Co at Kingston upon Thames in 1912 and went on to produce more than a dozen, largely undistinguished designs prior to the outbreak of war. The only one of note was the Bat Boat flying boat, the first biplane flying boat to be built in the UK, but this was to change with a series of very successful warplanes, beginning with the two-seat 1½ Strutter fighter, so named because of its unconventional wing strut arrangement. It entered service with the Royal Flying Corps and Royal Naval Air Service in the spring of 1916 and led to the development of the Pup, a smaller single-seat aircraft, of which 1,770 were built. Sopwith's Camel became the most successful British single-seat fighter of the war, serving between 1917 and the Armistice. A total of 5,490 were built with a number of different rotary engines. Other World War 1 types were the Triplane, a derivative of the Pup first flown on 28 May 1916; the Cuckoo torpedo-bomber and Dolphin fighter, both

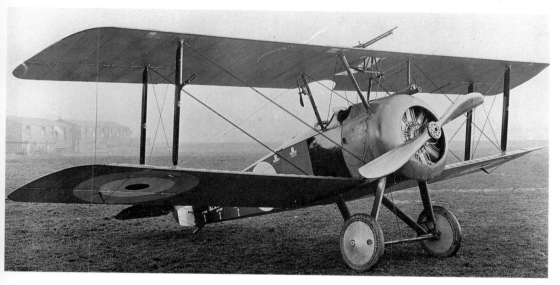

Above:
The two most famous British fighters of World War 1 were the SE5A and the Sopwith Camel, but the latter had greater firepower and shot down 1,294 enemy aircraft — claimed to be more than any other type. Developed from the Pup, it entered service in mid-1917. Total production reached 5,490 and Camels were supplied to the American Expeditionary Force (143), Belgium (36) and Greece (six).
M. J. Hooks Collection

Right:
The Sopwith Pup rapidly earned a good reputation for ease of handling, and production aircraft were available from September 1916 for the RNAS and RFC. Some 1,770 were built with engines from 80 to 100hp. Shown are airworthy examples of the Pup and the Sopwith Snipe, successor to the Camel, owned by Canada's National Aeronautical Collection. Over 500 Snipes were built.
M. J. Hooks Collection

making their aerial début in the spring of 1917; and the Bentley BR2-powered Snipe fighter and its ground-attack variant, the Salamander. Both just made it into service before the end of the war, and the Snipe became the standard RAF single-seat fighter in the postwar period until replaced by the Gloster Grebe and Armstrong Whitworth Siskin in 1923. The Sopwith Dragon, a 1919 development of the Snipe, never entered service. In the same year, the company produced several light aircraft for touring and competition flying, including the two-seat Grasshopper, Wallaby, Antelope and Dove; the single-seat Schneider, Rainbow and Scooter models, and the three-seat Gnu cabin aircraft. A heavy tax bill, however, forced the famous company, renamed The Sopwith Aviation & Engineering Co Ltd in June 1919, into liquidation in September 1920.

Southern

In August 1929, F. G. Miles, later to found his own manufacturing company, took to the air in a single-engine aerobatic biplane, based on the Avro Baby and built at Shoreham, Sussex, by Southern Aircraft Ltd. After the 85hp ABC Hornet flat-four was replaced by the 80hp Armstrong Siddeley Genet II radial, the type was named Martlet. Five more, all differing slightly, were built and followed by the Metal Martlet in 1931.

Top:
G-AAYX was the only Martlet to have a 100hp Armstrong Siddeley Genet Major engine. It started life as the personal mount of F. G. Miles and ended up in the Shuttleworth Collection at Old Warden in 1973.
Philip Jarrett Collection

Above:
The Spartan Cruiser appeared in 1932 and 16 of various versions were built with engines of 120 to 130hp, including one licence-built in Yugoslavia which had bought two Spartan-built examples. Others were exported to Iraq, Egypt and India (one each) and Czechoslovakia where two were operated by the Bata company. Illustrated is the second Mk III of Spartan Air Lines operating the Cowes-Heston service.
M. J. Hooks Collection

Spartan

Between 1928 and 1930, Simmonds Aircraft Ltd, owned by O. E. (later Sir Oliver) Simmonds, built 49 Spartan two-seater wooden biplanes at Weston, Southampton. After the company moved operations to East Cowes on the Isle of Wight and was reorganised as Spartan Aircraft Ltd, a new two-seater, the Arrow, was built, which incorporated many of the inter-changeable components, such as wing, rudder and undercarriage sections, of the original Simmonds design. The larger, unimaginatively styled Three Seater I and II came next, but Spartan's most attractive aircraft was the Cruiser, a sleek, three-engined 10-seat commercial monoplane, developed from the Saro-Percival Mailplane of 1931. The Cruiser was built in three versions (I, II and III), with a variety of 130hp engines, and saw service in Europe and the Middle East. Production of the Cruiser, the last type to be built by Spartan, ceased in May 1935 after the completion of 16 aircraft. The Pobjoy R-powered two-seater Clipper prototype was another type built at East Cowes in 1932.

Supermarine

Supermarine's history goes back to before World War 1, when Noel Pemberton-Billing began aircraft design and construction at Woolston, Southampton on 27 June 1914, beginning with the Supermarine PB1. A year later he formed Pemberton-Billing Ltd, renamed as the Supermarine Aviation Works Ltd in late 1916. In between these changes, he designed a number of types, including the PB9 scout, the PB23 and PB25 pusher fighters, and the PB29 anti-airship aircraft which led to the PB31 Night Hawk. The first Supermarine products were the four-seat Channel I and II flying boats, developed from the AD patrol boat of 1916. Staying largely with flying boats and amphibious aircraft, Supermarine produced in the following years the Sea Lion (1919), Seagull III (1921), Sea Eagle (1923) and the Southampton in 1925. The Seagull and Southampton, as well as the 1933 Seagull V, later renamed the Walrus, were all used on reconnaissance duties. The amphibious Sea Otter supplemented the Walrus during the war years. The Scapa, powered by two 525hp Rolls-Royce Kestrel IIIS radials, was an all-metal development of the Southampton, which entered RAF service in 1935, followed a year later by the Stranraer, a long-range reconnaissance and bombing flying boat. A single all-metal, six-seat flying boat, the Air Yacht, plied the Irish lakes on pleasure cruises.

Below:
Supermarine built two Sea Lion single-seat racing seaplanes, the first, G-EALP, for the 1919 Schneider Trophy Race which was declared void. The second, G-EBAH, won the 1922 race at Naples and was later rebuilt to come third in the 1923 race at Cowes at 151mph on its 450hp Napier Lion engine.
M. J. Hooks Collection

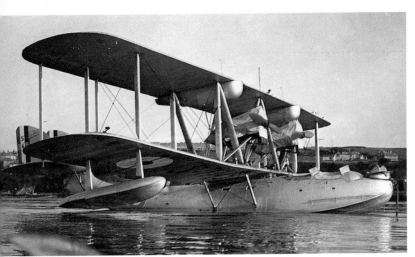

Left:
The Supermarine Southampton was a very successful flying boat, ordered for the RAF off the drawing board, and deliveries began in the summer of 1925. Some 20 Mk 1s had wooden hulls, but most were converted to metal-hulled Mk 2s. Production totalled 83 including four prototypes; overseas deliveries were made to Turkey (six), Argentina (eight), Australia (two), and Japan and Denmark (one each).

Above:
The Supermarine Stranraer entered RAF service in 1936 and served with home-based squadrons only, eventually being replaced by Sunderlands. Eighteen were built by Supermarine and a further 40 by Canadian Vickers in Montreal for the RCAF. Fourteen were subsequently civilianised and four went to the Canadian Queen Charlotte Airlines. CF-RXO illustrated was one of these and is preserved in the RAF Museum as RCAF 920, its original serial.
M. J. Hooks Collection

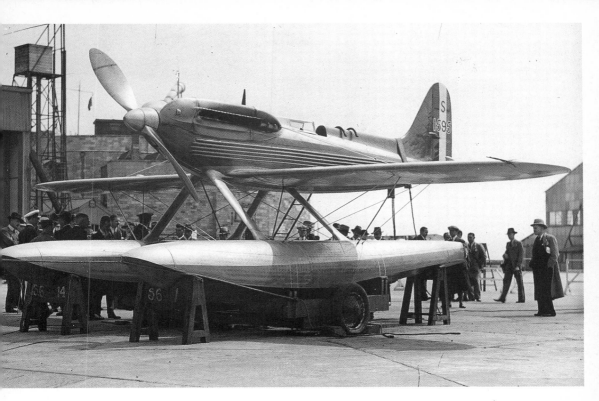

Supermarine also achieved success in the Schneider Trophy races with its S4, S5, S6 and S6B seaplanes, all designed by R. J. Mitchell, but failed in the Lympne Trials with the two-seat Sparrow. Mitchell's greatest triumph, however, was the Spitfire. The prototype made its début on 5 March 1936, powered by the new Rolls-Royce Merlin engine, and went on to serve during the war as a highly successful front-line fighter, fighter-bomber and on photo-reconnaissance duties, its many versions adding up to a production run in excess of 20,000 aircraft. The Seafire was a naval version with folding wings for carrier-borne operations which served until 1952, but the Spiteful and Seafang, direct descendants of the Spitfire and Seafire respectively, were cancelled at the end of hostilities. Postwar Supermarine products included the experimental SRA/1, the world's first turbojet-powered flying boat which flew on 16 July 1947; the Scimitar, a single-seat carrier-borne

Above:
Last of the line of Schneider Trophy racing seaplanes designed by R. J. Mitchell was the Supermarine S6B, two of which were built for the 1931 event. Withdrawal of opposing teams meant that the British merely had to fly over the course to win the Trophy outright, which they did averaging 340mph in S1595 illustrated. The same day, S1596 captured the world's Absolute Speed Record at 379mph. *M. J. Hooks Collection*

interceptor and strike aircraft; and the Swift, a single-seat swept-wing fighter, powered by the Rolls-Royce Avon turbojet. The company, which had become a division of Vickers-Armstrongs Ltd in October 1938 under the long-winded title of Vickers-Armstrongs Ltd (Aircraft Section) (Supermarine Division), became part of British Aircraft Corporation upon its establishment on 1 July 1960.

Trago Mills

In the early 1980s, Trago Mills Ltd, a large retailer based at Bodmin in Cornwall, built a superb two-seat aerobatic primary trainer known as the SAH-1. It was designed by Sydney A. Holloway and flew for the first time on 23 August 1983. However, no production orders were forthcoming and the company sold its aviation division to Orca Aircraft Ltd in August 1988. Orca did no better and folded a year later. The

Left:
Affectionately remembered by hundreds of aircrew rescued in its air-sea rescue role, the Supermarine Walrus first flew in June 1933 as the Seagull V and 741 were built for the RAF and FAA. Powerplant was a 775hp Bristol Pegasus driving a pusher propeller. One is being restored to airworthy condition, while static restorations can be seen in the RAF and FAA Museums.

Above:
Little justice can be done in a caption of Supermarine's most famous aircraft, the Spitfire. There are discrepancies in various records concerning production, but at least 20,400 of 22 versions were built, plus more than 2,000 Seafires; a number of Spitfires were also converted to Seafires. Spitfire IIA P7350 illustrated, the oldest surviving of a number of airworthy examples, flies with the Battle of Britain Memorial Flight.

design and manufacturing rights were then acquired by FLS Lovaux in October 1991, which flew the first production model on 16 December 1993. Two versions were offered, the basic Club Sprint with a 118hp Lycoming piston engine, and the Sprint 160, an enhanced variant with a more powerful 160hp Textron Lycoming engine. In order to concentrate on its core business of heavy aircraft maintenance, FLS is now looking for a buyer for the Sprint (and the Optica), and this excellent aircraft may well be built abroad.

Vickers

Among the earliest designs of Vickers Ltd (Aviation Department) was the EFB (Experimental Fighting Biplane) pusher of 1913, which led to many more army pushers, including the FB5 (Fighting Biplane No 5) and the improved and faster FB9. A total of 241 FB5s, nicknamed the Gunbus, were supplied to the Royal Flying Corps for frontline service, joined in the summer of 1916 by 95 FB9s. Smaller quantities were produced of the FB14 reconnaissance biplane and the FB19 single-seat fighter. During wartime, the Vickers factories at Brooklands, Weybridge, Surrey and at Crayford, Bexley Heath and Erith on the south-eastern outskirts of London, were kept busy building large numbers of BE2s, SE5as and Sopwith 1½ Strutters, as well as several prototypes of its own. A requirement for a strategic bomber produced the twin-engined FB27, which flew for the first time on 30 November 1917. This three-bay biplane with twin fins and rudders, later renamed Vimy, came too late for operational service in the war, but is remembered

for its pioneering long-distance flights in peacetime. Derivatives were the Vimy Commercial, the Vernon military transport, Victoria and Valentia 22-troop transports, and the larger Virginia bomber. The five-seat Viking amphibious biplane, powered by a 375hp Rolls-Royce Eagle pusher, was produced in 1919.

Other designs which made it into production included the two-seat Valparaiso and Vixen fighter/reconnaissance biplanes of 1924/25; the all-metal Vildebeest torpedo-carrying and bombing biplane, which entered RAF service in 1933, and the Vincent, a three-seat general purpose version of the Vildebeest, in RAF service from 1934. Vickers had also been building airships since 1908, culminating in the R100, designed by B. N. (later Sir Barnes) Wallis and N. S. Norway (later novelist Nevil Shute). In August 1928, the aviation department became Vickers (Aviation) Ltd, which three months later took over Supermarine, although the latter retained its identity. Barnes Wallis devised the geodetic form of construction, based on airship stressing combining extreme light weight with great strength, and this was applied for the first time in the Wellesley bomber, flown on

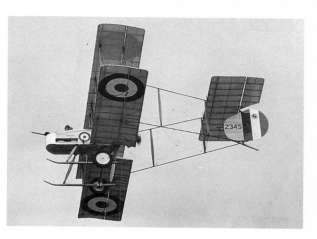

19 June 1935 and powered by a single Bristol Pegasus radial piston engine, and the twin-engined prototype, which first flew on 15 June 1936 and led to the Wellington bomber. Between 1936 and the end of 1945, Vickers built 11,461 Wellingtons in several versions, more than any other British aircraft with the exception of the Spitfire and Hurricane. The Wellington was followed by the slightly larger Warwick, adapted for reconnaissance duties with Coastal Command in 1943, and after the war by the four-engined Valiant high-altitude strategic bomber, the first of the RAF's V-bombers to enter service in January 1955.

On 22 June 1945, Vickers flew the 24-27 seat Viking short-haul airliner, fitted with two 1,675hp Bristol Hercules radials, and went on to build 161 Vikings and 426 Valetta military transports and Varsity crew trainers at Weybridge and Hurn Airport, Bournemouth. Even greater success was achieved with the 65-seat four-engined Viscount, the world's first turboprop transport to enter airline service. The V630 prototype flew on 16 July 1948 and was superseded by the improved V700 and V800 Series, production ending in 1964 after 445 units. Its successor, the larger V950 Vanguard, had already been overtaken by the jet age when it flew on 20 January 1959, and only 43 were built. Development and production of the four-engined, turbofan-powered VC10 airliner, whose origins went back to the cancelled V1000 project of the mid-1950s, was continued by the British Aircraft Corporation in which Vickers-Armstrongs (Aircraft) Ltd, so named after reorganisation in December 1954, became a 40% shareholder in February 1960.

Above:
The Vickers Vildebeest torpedo bomber replaced the RAF's Hawker Horsleys and entered service in 1933. Total production amounted to 194. Nos 36 and 100 Sqn put up a valiant fight against the Japanese at Singapore in 1943. A modified version (illustrated) was named Vincent and 171 were built, replacing Westland Wapitis and Fairey IIIFs. *M. J. Hooks Collection*

Left:
Vickers' R100 airship flew in December 1929 and was powered by six 670hp Rolls-Royce engines. It flew to Canada and back in July/August 1930, but following the loss of the rival R101 at Beauvais the airship programme was stopped and R100 was scrapped.

Left:
Most numerous of RAF bombers for the first three years of World War 2, the Vickers Wellington, with its unusual Barnes Wallis-designed geodetic construction, proved capable of withstanding heavy damage. A few had Rolls-Royce Merlin engines but the vast majority of the 11,461 built had either 1,000hp Bristol Pegasus or 1,500hp Bristol Hercules engines. A Wellington II with Merlins is shown. *M. J. Hooks Collection*

Above:
Designed to replace the Wellington, the Vickers Warwick was of similar construction, but with the advent of the four-engine bombers it was not required in that role and was transferred to air-sea rescue and general reconnaissance. Total production was 509; 14 were transferred to BOAC as transports on North African and Mediterranean routes and the first of these is shown.

Below:
Vickers' first postwar airliner was the Viking, which entered service with BEA in 1946. A total of 161 were built, and many were exported. A military version, the Valetta, entered RAF service in 1948 replacing Dakotas. The Vickers Varsity was a further development with a tricycle undercarriage, used for crew training

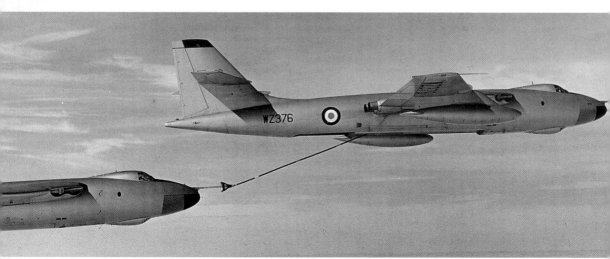

Westland

The Westland Aircraft Works were established on the West Hendford site at Yeovil in 1915 as a subsidiary of engine manufacturers, Petters Ltd, becoming Westland Aircraft Ltd in July 1935. Concentrating initially on building aircraft under subcontract, it also developed three designs of its own during the war years. These were the N1B single-seat Scout seaplane, the small Wagtail single-seat fighter, and the two-seat Weasel, intended as a replacement for the Bristol F2B. The Limousine, first flown in July 1919, was Westland's first commercial aircraft, seating three passengers in a comfortable enclosed cabin, and was followed by the two-seat Woodpigeon biplane in summer 1924 and the similarly-sized Widgeon parasol monoplane, first flown on 22 September that same year. Other civil models were the Westland IV and Wessex four-seat high-wing feeder aircraft, which went into airline service in 1929/30. Military designs in the 1920s comprised the Walrus, a three-seat carrier-borne spotter biplane flown in 1920, the Yeovil long-range day bomber, Wizard single-seat monoplane fighter, Westbury three-seat twin-engined biplane fighter and the Wapiti, a two-seat general purpose biplane, first flown in March 1927 and normally powered by the 480hp Bristol Jupiter VIII engine. The Wallace was an improved Wapiti with a Bristol Pegasus engine. Westland also became involved in a series of tail-less aircraft, known as Pterodactyls and designed by Captain G. T. R. Hill.

The Lysander two-seat army co-operation monoplane, affectionately known as Lizzie during the war, made its maiden flight on 15 June 1936 and entered RAF service in June 1938. The initial Lysander I was powered by a 890hp Bristol Mercury XII radial engine, replaced in the Mk II by the 905hp Bristol Perseus XII, and in the Mk III by a Mercury 30. During World War 2, Westland also built the Whirlwind single-seat, twin-engine, heavily-armed fighter, the Fairey Barracuda and 2,200 Spitfire and Seafire aircraft, but the twin-engine high-altitude Welkin never became operational. The single-seat Wyvern naval strike aircraft appeared on its first flight on 12 December 1946 and entered service with the Royal Navy in 1953. It was the company's last fixed-wing design, before going over to helicopter manufacture. Beginning with licence production of several Sikorsky designs, including the S-51 as the Dragonfly, later redeveloped into the five-seat Widgeon, the S-55 as the Whirlwind and S-58 as the Wessex, Westland also built the Agusta-Bell 47G-3B for the British Army as the Sioux. Development of the 40-passenger, or six-tonne payload Westminster helicopter, flown in prototype form on 15 June 1958, was abandoned two years later.

Top left:
Earning the distinction of being the world's first turbine-engined airliner, the Vickers Viscount still holds the record for British airliner production with 445 built. BEA operated the first scheduled service with the prototype in July 1950, and larger variants followed. More than 60 operators in 40 countries acquired new Viscounts, and others eventually bought pre-owned aircraft. All Viscounts were powered by Rolls-Royce Dart engines. *M. J. Hooks Collection*

Centre left:
Designed as a larger successor to the Viscount, the Vickers Vanguard, with seating for 93 passengers, did not achieve the same success, although the production aircraft for BEA (20) and Trans Canada Airlines (23) served the companies well. A few BEA Vanguards were converted to Merchantman freighters.

Left:
First of the RAF's three types of V-bomber to fly was the Vickers Valiant in May 1951. Deliveries began in January 1955 and eventually totalled 79. The V-bombers' role change to low-level operations in 1964 resulted in Valiants being withdrawn the following year with main spar fatigue, but some were converted to tankers as shown. *M. J. Hooks Collection*

Right:
Westland experimented with a series of Pterodactyl designs in the 1920/30s. The three-seat Mk 1V illustrated flew in March 1931 with a 120hp DH Gipsy III engine but only one other Pterodactyl, the Mk 1V two-seat fighter design, followed. *M. J. Hooks Collection*

Top:
First flown on 22 February 1929, the Westland Wessex carried a crew of two and four passengers. Ten were built, including the prototype; four went to SABENA, one to the Egyptian Government, three to Imperial Airways, one to Portsmouth, Southsea & Isle of Wight Airways, and one to Sir Alan Cobham's National Aviation Day Displays, which also received two from SABENA. *M. J. Hooks Collection*

Above:
The RAF's first army-co-operation monoplane, the Westland Lysander, entered service in June 1938 and the 1,427 built in Britain were used in many other roles including air-sea rescue, agent dropping and target towing. A further 225 were built in Canada. Foreign operators included Turkey (36), France (23), USA (25), Egypt (19), Finland, Portugal (eight) and Ireland (six), some being ex-RAF stocks. *M. J. Hooks Collection*

Right:
After considerable teething troubles, the Westland Wyvern strike aircraft joined the Royal Navy in May 1953. A lengthy test programme followed the flight of the first prototype in December 1946; the first 15 aircraft had Rolls-Royce Eagle piston engines but subsequent versions had 4,110ehp Armstrong Siddeley Python turboprops. Around 120 were built; illustrated are Wyvern S4 of No 813 Sqn based at Ford in 1953. *M. J. Hooks Collection*

When the 1957 Defence White Paper signalled the reorganisation of the aviation industry, Westland saw its opportunity to become the UK's leading helicopter manufacturer and acquired Saunders-Roe in 1959, the Bristol Helicopter Division on 23 March 1960, and the UK aviation interests of Fairey Aviation Ltd, in the process acquiring factories at East Cowes, Eastleigh, Hayes and Weston-super-Mare. From Bristol came the Belvedere 19-troop transport, from Fairey the Rotodyne (abandoned in 1962) and the Gannet fixed-wing naval strike and anti-submarine aircraft, and from Saunders-Roe the P531 five-seat

Top:
Interest by the Royal Navy in the Saunders-Roe P531 prototypes led to the Westland Wasp and Scout series of helicopters; the first Wasp flew in October 1962 and the type entered service in June 1963. They operated from frigates, Commando carriers and short bases and more than 100 were built. New Wasps were supplied to Brazil, The Netherlands, New Zealand and South Africa, and the first three countries also received a number of refurbished aircraft.

Above:
The Westland Belvedere, originally designed by Bristol as the Type 192, was the RAF's first tandem-rotor helicopter. Powered by two 1,300shp Napier Gazelle turboprops, it entered service in September 1961 and saw action in Tanganyika, Arabia and Borneo. Only 26 were built and the type was retired in 1967.
M. J. Hooks Collection

Top:
The Westland 30 was developed using Lynx components in the rotors, etc and flew in April 1979. Forty
were built, of which 21 went to India where the fleet
was grounded after three fatal accidents. Various
engines from 1,135 to 2,100shp were fitted, but the
production line was finally closed early in 1988.

Above:
A pre-production batch of nine three-engined EH101
helicopters was laid down by Westland and Italian
company Agusta between 1984 and 1990. Westland
assembled Nos 1, 3, 4, 5 and 8, and Agusta Nos 2, 6,
7 and 9. The first EH101 flew in October 1987 and
No 9 in January 1991. Development continues; G-0101
illustrated is a civil variant, the Heliliner.
M. J. Hooks Collection

Overleaf:
The Lynx, a fast military helicopter for general purpose
and naval roles, was one of three types of helicopters
covered by the Anglo-French agreement of April 1968.
Nearly 400 have been sold to date. The Super Lynx,
shown here in service with the Portuguese Navy as the
Mk95, is an updated export version.

general purpose helicopter, developed by Westland into the Scout for the British Army and into the Wasp, used in an anti-submarine role by the Royal Navy. The Sea King family was developed from the Sikorsky SH-3D to a Royal Navy requirement for an advanced anti-submarine helicopter with all-weather capability. The first production version flew on 7 May 1969 and more than 250 have been built to date, including the Commando, a tactical variant first flown on 12 September 1973. The twin Rolls-Royce Gem-powered Lynx multi-purpose medium helicopter based on the original Westland WG13 design, is one of three types covered by the Anglo-French helicopter agreement of 2 April 1968. Westland has design leadership in the Lynx programme and has produced in a variety of versions, including the uprated Super Lynx and Battlefield Lynx export models, as well as the five-seat Gazelle helicopter, also part of the Anglo-French agreement.

A venture into the commercial market with the 19-seat twin-engined Westland 30, originally known as the WG30 and first flown on 10 April 1979 using many Lynx components, proved less successful, only 41 being built. Present development work comprises the large 30-seat three-engined EH101, jointly with

Agusta of Italy. Designed as a multi-role helicopter, the first EH101 prototype flew at Yeovil on 9 October 1987 and the Royal Navy EH101 Merlin, powered by three 2,312shp Rolls-Royce Turbomeca RTM 322 turboshaft engines, is due to enter service in 1999. Westland also produces a licence-version of the Sikorsky Black Hawk helicopter under the designation WS70L.

White and Thompson

Electrical engineer Norman A. Thompson and Dr Douglas White founded the White and Thompson Co Ltd in June 1912 to build aircraft. Its first was the No 1, a two-seater designed by F. W. Lanchester and powered by two 50hp Gnome engines, first assembled by the Daimler Motor Co in Coventry, but then transferred to its own premises at Middleton-on-Sea, near Bognor, Sussex. Thompson himself then designed the No 2 side-by-side pusher in 1913, fitted with a 120hp ABC engine. The No 3 was a two-seat anti-submarine flying boat, eight of which were delivered to the Royal Naval Air Service in 1915. In the same year, the RNAS also accepted 10 Bognor Bloater wooden biplanes, used on coastal patrol duties. After Norman Thompson struck out on his own, renaming the company Norman Thompson Flight Co on 4 October 1915, he designed and built several more types during the rest of World War 1, including 50 NT4, a reconnaissance and anti-submarine flying boat powered by two Hispano-Suiza engines and at least 150 NT2B flying boat trainers. The N1B fighter flying boat was built in prototype form only.

Evaluation by the Royal Navy of the de Havilland
Venom NF2 night fighter led to orders for the Sea
Venom FAW20. Total production amounted to 256
including some built in Australia and licence production
in France as the S. E. Aquilon. Shown is a Royal Navy
FAW21. *M. J. Hooks Collection*